Mary Francis Cusack

Advice to Irish girls in America

Mary Francis Cusack

Advice to Irish girls in America

ISBN/EAN: 9783744741224

Printed in Europe, USA, Canada, Australia, Japan

Cover: Foto ©Lupo / pixelio.de

More available books at **www.hansebooks.com**

ADVICE

TO

IRISH GIRLS IN AMERICA,

BY THE

NUN OF KENMARE,

(SISTER MARY FRANCIS CLARE.)

AUTHOR OF "ILLUSTRATED LIFE OF ST. PATRICK, APOSTLE OF IRELAND;" "JESUS AND JERUSALEM, OR, THE WAY HOME;" "LIFE AND REVELATIONS OF ST. GERTRUDE," &c., &c.

(TENTH THOUSAND.)

NEW YORK:
J. A. McGEE, PUBLISHER,
7 BARCLAY STREET.
1872.

Entered according to act of Congress in the year 1872, by
J. A. McGEE,
In the office of the Librarian of Congress at Washington.

CONTENTS.

CHAPTER I.

                                             PAGE

BEGIN AT THE BEGINNING 9
You who left dear Old Ireland and went to America 12
Legend of the Old Monk 13
How long the hours are in Hell—how short in Heaven 17

CHAPTER II.

HOW TO GET RICH 22
A rolling stone gathers no moss 27
Going to bad places of amusement 32
Story about St. Charles Borromeo 36
The devil is always busy 40
The rich man and the poor beggar 43

CHAPTER III.

	PAGE
THE HONOR OF BEING SERVANTS	47
How long will money and rank last?	51
Money will not keep away death or sickness	54

CHAPTER IV.

SOME ADVICE ABOUT DIFFERENT DUTIES WHICH WE MAY HAVE TO DO	60
Our Guardian Angel	61
Be content with your situation in life	64
What St. Paul says to servants	67
Advice about minding children	70
Story of St. Aloysius, the holy Jesuit	75

CHAPTER V.

SAME SUBJECT, CONTINUED	79
What is prayer?	79
On getting up in the morning	82
Short Prayer for the morning	88
The girl who gets up late in the morning	90

CHAPTER VI.

ADVICE ABOUT HONESTY	94
Wasting food	96
Stealing money, jewels or dress	100

CONTENTS. v

CHAPTER VII.
PAGE

Advice about temptations 103
How the devil tempts you 106
Do not listen for a single moment to temptation.. 111

CHAPTER VIII.

Advice about prayer and the sacraments 115
Advice about prayer 117
The great famine in Ireland 120
On the sacraments 122
Baptism 123
Confirmation 124
Eucharist 125
Penance 127

CHAPTER IX.

Advice on the sacraments, continued 134
Extreme Unction 134
Holy Orders 142
Matrimony 145
Unhappy marriages 146
Do not marry a man given to drink 147
Be good wives 149

CHAPTER X.

Advice about good example 151
Modesty in dress 153
Protestants arguing about religion 155

	PAGE
Catholics at service in Protestant families	160
What happened in my own family	165
Eating meat on Friday	170

CHAPTER XI.

POINTS OF CONTROVERSY BETWEEN CATHOLICS AND PROTESTANTS	173
The holy Apostles were Catholics	175
The Catholic Church has never changed	179
Luther, the founder of the Protestant religion	183
God gave the Saints power to work miracles	187
Protestants believe in table-turning and spirit-rapping	191

CHAPTER XII.

ADVICE ABOUT DEVOTIONS TO OUR BLESSED LADY	193
Wear the Scapular	197
"Pray for me and I will pray for you. I have prayed for every one who reads this little book."	198
The Pope's Letter to the Sister	199

ADVICE
TO
YOUNG CATHOLIC WOMEN.

CHAPTER I.

BEGIN AT THE BEGINNING.

THERE is no one in the world, however learned, or however holy, who may not be the better for "Good Advice." It is only foolish people who won't listen to advice; wise people know very well that, however much they may know, there are other people who know more; you know that when people wish to excel in any one art or science, they give their whole minds to that one subject. If a man wishes to become a good painter, he spends all his time learning the art of painting, and how to blend and mix his colors. If a man wishes to become a first-rate carpenter, he sets himself to learn his trade from some one who is very skillful at it.

My children, people are very wise and very prudent when they wish to learn how to get on in this world, that is, when they wish to learn how to be rich, or clever, or respected, for the next fifty or sixty years; but after that—my children, after that, they die, or they become incapable of working any longer. Their friends pity them; if they are fond of them they take care of them, and keep them until they die, and then they say, "Thank God they are gone." If they do not care for them, if they have been bad, selfish men, they are glad to get rid of them, and there is the end.

Do you think that worth living for? What about the twenty, and thirty, and fifty, and a hundred hundred thousand years of ETERNITY? It is certainly very pleasant to be thought a great deal about in this world, and to have all our friends very fond of us, and to hear people praise us, and to have a bag of dollars, and have a great funeral when we die; but after that? My children, do we think what will come after? Listen a little, and I will tell you. Try if you can count the stars up in the sky some bright winter night; you will soon stop, there are so many. Try if you can count all the leaves on the first tree you see. That will be still more difficult. Well, my children, if you counted all the stars and all the leaves fifty thousand times over, and then fifty thousand times more, you would only be at the beginning of ETERNITY—of that *life* about which I am going to give you good advice.

Many of you left dear old Ireland, and went out to America, the Land of the Free, where labor gets its reward, in this world at least. Do you remember how anxious you were to know all about America before you went there?

You asked all the neighbors who had friends out there what they said about it, and what place was best to go to, and how you could get your passage the cheapest way, and what clothes you should take, and what wages you would get when you went out there. You were never done asking questions, and you were quite right too; it was your duty to get all the information you could.

And then some of you who were born out in America, when you wanted to place yourselves out in the world, did you not also make every inquiry, and ask which was the best house to go to service in, and what kind the people were?

And so it is that we are very wise indeed for this world, and take care to get the best place we can, and the best payment we can for our work, and quite right too.

But, my children, if we take all this trouble for what can only last but for a a few years, how much trouble ought we not to take for what will last for thousands and thousands of years!

There is a story or legend told of an old monk who went to take a walk one summer evening in a wood away from his convent. He was a holy old man, and he had given up all his time and thoughts to prepare for the other world, as all monks and nuns should do. God has diffcrent ways of preparing people for Heaven, and this was His way. Your way is to work for Him in the world, but I shall say more about this later on.

Well, the good old monk had his heart full of holy thoughts, and as he walked on he was admiring the beauty of the flowers and the beauty of the trees, and the beauty of the birds, and he thought to himself, after all, that there was a great deal of pleasure and variety in this world, and he wondered, just for a little while, how Heaven could be happier or more beautiful; and he wondered, too, would people ever get tired of Heaven—would they be weary even of its pleasures, as one is so often weary of the pleasures of this world.

After a little, he heard a bird singing. He stopped to listen. He had never heard anything like it. He stopped a little longer. Indeed, the music was so beautiful, so heavenly, he could not go on.

At last the bird stopped singing. He hastened back to the monastery, for though he thought he had only listened to it for about a quarter of an hour, he saw it was getting very late. The sun was set, the moon was up, the bright stars had come out in the evening sky.

He soon reached his monastery, but all seemed strangely changed. He thought at first it was the dark shades of evening that had made everything appear so different, that had made the young shrubs appear like old trees, and the new, beautiful monastery so dark and ancient looking.

An old monk came and opened the great door of the convent and asked who he was. This seemed still more wonderful; he could not tell who the old monk was, and the old monk could not tell who he was. Then some other monks came, but he did not know any of them—all was changed. They asked his name, and he told them, but they could not remember any person of that name.

The superior of the monastery looked in the great book where all the names of the monks were entered, and they found his name. A hundred years had passed away since it had been entered there, and they had put down that he had left the monastery one summer evening and had never returned, and no one knew what had become of him.

Then he understood all.

He told the good Father Prior; and the monks knew he had been all that time listening to the song of a bird, and how it seemed to him as if he had been only away from the monastery for a few minutes; and he knew now that the good God had allowed this to happen in order that he might know that a hundred years in Heaven would only seem like a few minutes, because of the great and wonderful happiness which we shall enjoy there.

My children, is it not worth our while to prepare ourselves for this wonderful and blessed home, where we shall have everything we can possibly desire? We shall never feel hunger nor thirst, nor wet nor cold; where we shall never want money nor clothing, or rest, or sleep; where we shall never even shed a tear, or heave a sigh, or have a wish ungratified; and all this is to last forever, forever and ever, forever and ever.

The story I have told you about the monk may not be literally true. It was probably only a dream or parable, but it will help us to understand that which is certainly true.

But we all know ourselves how quick the time passes when we are enjoying ourselves, when we are with friends whom we are fond of, when we listen to some amusing conversation, or some beautiful music. You will often hear people say on such occasions, "I had no idea it was so late;" and at other times, when we are in great pain, or suffering, or trouble, how slow the time goes; when we are very, very ill in the night we say to ourselves, "I wonder will it ever be day?" When we are tossing about on the sea, and very sick, we say, "How long the days are!" but the time is neither longer nor shorter, the change is in ourselves. When we are unhappy, an hour seems like three hours; when we are merry, an hour seems like five minutes; but the hour is just the same, neither longer nor shorter.

My children, let us think how long the hours will seem in hell, and how short they will seem in heaven; let us think a great deal about this.

Hundreds of people, yes, I ought to say thousands of people, are lost because they will not think.

They are too busy to think, or too careless to think. What should you think of a man who said he was too busy to mind his business? Why, you would laugh at him; you would say, what a fool he is; you would say, if he does not keep his store, his store won't keep him. If he does not mind his business, no one else will mind it for him.

My children, we have only one real business in this world, and that is to prepare ourselves for heaven. If we mind that business, we are all right; if we neglect that business, we are worse than fools; we are poor and miserable creatures, even if we possessed more dollars than any one in the world.

But you must not misunderstand me; you must not suppose that you are to neglect your business in this world in order to secure your happiness in the next; you must not suppose that you may not try to make money honestly in this world in order to be rich in the next. The advice I am going to give you will, I hope, help you in this world as well as in the next. Pray to God, and to the blessed Virgin Mary, the Mother of Jesus, that you may be wise both for Time and Eternity.

CHAPTER II.

HOW TO GET RICH.

I suppose there is no one in the world who does not wish to be rich. Indeed, there are some people who think of nothing else but how they can add dollar to dollar. Some persons seem to love money for its own sake, and to like to have it for the very pleasure of looking at it. They are misers, and you know no one respects or cares for a miser. The more money they have the more they wish for, and the more unhappy they are.

Instead of being glad that they have so

much, they are very unhappy, for they are always wishing for more. If they reach ten thousand dollars, they would wish for twenty thousand. If they had twenty thousand dollars, they would be miserable because they had not got thirty thousand.

Poor people! they are very much to be pitied; their money does them no good in this world, and when they die they cannot take it away with them; they must leave it here after them, and even if they could take it with them, and could take it to Heaven with them, who would care for it, and of what use would it be to them?

Very often the miser will starve himself. There was a man died in Cork the other day of cold and hunger, and yet he had no less than two hundred pounds in the bank. Every one said "What a fool he was!" but for all that, there will always be persons who are equally foolish.

Perhaps if any one had spoken to him about this—if a good priest had known of it, and had told him how foolish and how sinful his conduct was, the man would have said; "My money is my own, and I have a right to do what I like with it."

My children, we have nothing of our own in this sense. We have the power, certainly, to do what we like with our time and our money, because the good God has given us all a free will, so that we can do as we please; but we have no right to commit sin, and this poor man was committing sin.

Everything we have belongs to God, because God has given us everything. He gives us our health, and our time, and our memory, and our intellect, but he gives us these things for His glory, and that we may use them for His service, and not that we may use them for the devil.

There are some persons who are very anxious to get rich, because they like to have plenty of money to spend. The miser likes the money for its own sake; he likes to look at his gold just for the sinful, selfish pleasure of hoarding it up, and thinking that he has it; but some people like money for the sake of what they can get for it. They like money for the value that it gets for them; now there may be no harm in this and there may be a great deal of harm.

If a girl wishes to have money that she may keep herself respectable, or better her position in life, and if she does not take any wrong means to get this money, and is not sinfully anxious about it, this is no harm.

But if she wishes to be rich that she may buy fine clothes, which are not suitable to her station in life, or that she may be able to go to places of amusement which are sinful, and where she may see and hear wickedness, which no Catholic girls should see or hear, then she is doing very wrong, and is putting herself in danger both in this world and the next.

There are very few people who are really content with what they have. But there are degrees in discontent as there are dangers in sin. You know, however, that a little poison is a bad thing; what would you say to a person who took some poison and said: "Oh, it has a nice taste, and I am sure a little cannot do me any great harm; at all events, I will try it."

Would it not be a great deal wiser and better to have nothing to do with it? And so the wisest way is to try to be content with what God has given us.

If a girl has a good situation, with a good master and mistress, if she is where she can attend regularly to her religious duties, I do not think she is wise to leave her place to go to another from whom she may get more wages. There is an old saying, "That a rolling stone will never gather moss." It means that if one is always changing one gets no good by it, though we may fancy we do.

When a girl stays a long time in one family she gets attached to her master and mistress, and they get attached to her. They will do many things for her, and help her in sickness and trouble, which no stranger would do. Yet there is no harm in changing a place to better one's self; only people should be quite sure that they are bettering themselves, and that they are not going further to fare worse.

Sometimes it might be right to make a change when you could, where you would get more wages. If you have a father and mother, or other relatives, depending upon you, whom you ought to support, or if you are engaged to be married, and want to lay by something for your future home, then you would be quite right to try to make a little money; but take care you do not set your heart on it.

There is no harm in itself in having money, or in wishing to make or earn money; the harm is in caring for it more than we care for God, who has told us that we must not love the world, or the things of the world, and that the love of money is the source of all evil.

How many unhappy people have been tempted to commit suicide, to commit murder, to rob their employers, all from this wretched love and desire of money. A love of money is almost like a love of drink. When this desire once possesses a person he can never rest; he cries out like the drunkard, "More, more!" he will do anything to get more.

Try, then, honestly and religiously, to get on in the world, but remember there is another world, and that it is of a great deal more consequence to get on well there.

Shall I tell you the secret of being rich both here and hereafter?

My children, would it be wise for us to lay by a great deal of money this year if we knew that we would not enjoy one cent of it next year? But if you are wise you may enjoy your money both in this world and in the next.

You know that God will judge us at the last Great Day for every thought, and word, and action; there is no thought so secret that God does not know it. You may say to yourself, sometimes, "My thoughts are my own; no one can know what I am thinking. People may guess at it, may say, 'I guess I know what you are thinking of;' but they can only 'guess,' they cannot be sure."

My children, there is ONE who knows every thought you are thinking all day long; every moment of your life you are thinking, from the moment you awake in the morning until the moment you go to sleep at night you are thinking. God knows and reads every one of these thoughts as plain and plainer than you can read this book. God will judge you for all these thoughts. If they have been good thoughts He will reward you for them, if they have been bad thoughts, He will punish you.

All day long you are doing something; from the time you get up in the morning, until you go to bed at night, you are doing something. Those whom you live with can judge your actions to a certain extent, because they can see them; but they cannot judge them as God judges them, for they cannot see the motive of your action, they cannot tell the reason why you do certain things.

My children, it is very important that you should understand this well.

Suppose a servant girl wanted to go in

the evening to some bad place of amusement, where she knew that bad words would be said, and that there would be drinking, and swearing, and gambling, and bad dances; and that she got through her work all day very well, and very quick, that she might go to this place in the evening. Do you think she would be doing her work for a good motive?

But people who saw her so quick, and handy, and clever at her business might say, "What a good girl! I wish I had a help like her; see how much she does in such a short time, and so well, too!" You see, my children, this person could not know the girl's motive; she only saw the actions, and they looked very fair.

But God saw her heart. What do you think God thought of her work? Do you think God will give her a reward for that day's work? Would He not, on the contrary, punish her for it hereafter, unless, indeed, she repented for it before she died?

But she would get paid for it in this world? Certainly, her master and mistress would pay her for her work; but she would get nothing in the next world.

Now, I called this chapter "How to get Rich," because I want to show you how you can get paid in this world and in the next also.

My children, there are thousands of people who think only of what they can get for their work in this world; they never think at all about what they may get for it in the next. One feels so sorry for those people! There they are, working always like slaves all day long, and quite content with getting a little money, which, however useful and necessary, will all perish; and forgetting the wealth they might lay up where no one can ever steal it from them—where no fire can burn it—where no rust can spoil it.

My children, my dear, dear children, I want you to be very rich, I want you to begin from this very day to lay up treasures in the Bank of Heaven. When you and I die, and go to that happy place, as we may hope by God's mercy that we shall, then, perhaps, many of you will come to me and say: "Oh, look at my treasures—look how rich I am! how glad I am now that I listened to good advice, and laid up all this in the Bank of Heaven!"

My children, we shall only have one subject of regret, and that will be that we did not put more into that bank. And then, perhaps, by God's great mercy, we should go—you and I—and stand before God's great bright Throne, and sing an Alleluia of Praise and Thanksgiving for His Eternal Love—for His goodness to us poor sinners, in opening this Bank for us, and allowing us to lay up our treasures there.

Now suppose that, instead of hurrying her work for a bad purpose, this girl had said to herself, in the morning :

> My God, I offer Thee, this day,
> All I shall do, or think, or say ;
> Uniting it with what was done
> On earth, by Jesus Christ, Thy Son,

and that she had tried to do all her work well, to please God, as well as to please her mistress—oh, how rich she would be at night !

But you must not suppose that there is

any harm in innocent amusement. God does not wish us to live sad and lonely lives. He has given us a great many sources of enjoyment in this world, and we may see from this how much more He will give us, and do for us, in the next. You may please God, and have a reward in the next world even for the actions which you do for your pleasure. It is a pleasure to eat and drink; and we are told, in God's Holy Book, the Bible, that we not only may eat and drink for the glory of God, but that we ought to do so.

I will tell you a story, which is quite true, that will explain this better.

There is a saint, called St. Charles Borromeo. He was Archbishop of Milan, in Italy, for many years, and he devoted himself with his whole heart to the service of the poor; when there was a dreadful pestilence in that city he went about, day and night, among the people, trying to help and comfort them, and above all, giving them the last Sacrament.

My children, it will only be known in the Day of Judgment, how many priests have laid down their lives for the poor, like Jesus, the Good Shepherd—how many priests have been worn out with toil and labor for us poor sinners.

Well, this good and holy Bishop knew very well that people could not be all day on their knees praying, or all day attending the sick. Of course, in a time of great trouble, as for example when there was a plague, no one could think of anything but attending to the sick; but at other times he knew that people must have some recreation—some amusement, and so he sometimes played a game of chess with his friends.

One day while he was thus employed, those who were with him began to talk about death and the day of judgment, and they asked each other, "What would you like to be doing if you were called suddenly to the other world?" You may be sure a great many said they would like to be at their prayers; but what did the saint say? Well, he said he would be quite satisfied to die at this game of chess, for he began it for almighty God, and he would like when he died to be found doing God's will.

So you see the great thing for us is to be sure that we are doing God's will. If what we are doing is not sinful in itself, it matters little what it is. Certainly, if we could know we were going to die, we might wish to be making an act of contrition; no doubt this is what we should pray for, that God would grant us the grace to receive the sacraments, and to die with the full knowledge that we are dying and that we should soon be judged. But this incident in the life of the saint is to show us that we need not fear to die if we are in a state of grace, no matter what our employment may be, so long as it is innocent, and that we need not fear that God will be angry with us, or even be displeased with us for taking some amusement.

My children, God is not a hard master; the devil is the only hard master. He likes to make us commit sin, though he attempts to disguise sin to us, so as to make it look pleasant, yet we all know very well that sin never gives any real pleasure, even in this world, and we all know very well that sin will cause us everlasting pain and misery in the world to come.

Some people wish to be rich, as they say, for the sake of their families. Certainly it is the duty of a father and a mother to try and do their best to provide for their children, and it is the duty of a child to help her father and mother by her earnings as far as she can, if they want help.

But people sometimes make their duty an excuse for doing wrong. The devil is very busy; he is always trying to tempt us. He knows very well what he is about; he suits his temptations to our weakness.

He will go to the good father and mother, who are anxious, and rightly anxious, to provide for their children, and he will try to make them over-anxious. He will try to make them so anxious that they will commit the sin of distrusting God, or perhaps of taking sinful ways of enriching themselves.

He will go to some good girl, who is very anxious to do all she can for her parents, and he will tempt her to take some money, or some article of dress, or some food that does not belong to her; he will try to make her think that it is "no harm;" that her parents want it, and that the person that she takes it from does not want it, and will never miss it.

My children, the devil is very clever; do not listen to him, for if you do, you will be quite sure to repent it. Never listen to temptation. If you saw a lion coming up to you, would you stop to talk to it? Indeed, you would not, you would run away as fast as ever you could.

The devil is like a lion; the Bible calls him a "roaring lion," who is always going about to deceive us, and to try and make us do wrong. See how well he managed with Eve. He did not think he could get her to disobey God openly, so he said to her it was "no harm." Believe me, the most dangerous temptations arise in this way, the most dangerous faults come from listening to this kind of temptation. "It is no harm," says the devil. He knows very well it is harm, and great harm, but he was a liar from the beginning.

When you are tempted to do anything, and say to yourself, "perhaps it is no harm," stop at once, and ask yourself would you like your confessor to see you do it. What do you think he would say about it? If you think he would say, "don't do it," you may be quite sure it is wrong, and if you have any doubt, ask him next time you go to confession; remember it is better to be "sure than sorry," and remember that it is not only in this world, but in the next, that we shall be sorry for doing wrong.

My children, "goodness with contentment is great grace." Be content with the station in life in which which God has placed you. Be ever content with the money that you earn fairly and honestly, and remember that though you may be poor in this world, you may be very, very rich in the world to come.

We read in the holy gospels of a man of great wealth, who fared sumptuously every day, and dressed magnificently, and when he died he went to Hell. What good did all his fine clothes do him there? What good did all the riches he once had do him there? What advantage was it to him then that he had the most dainty food every day of his life on earth?

In Hell he wanted one drop of cold water, and could not get it. All his money could not buy him so much as one little drop of water. The poorest beggar on earth was better off.

And there was a poor beggar who used to lie at the rich man's door. He had scarcely enough of clothes to cover him; he could only get but food enough to keep him alive, and food of the very worst kind; when he was ill he had no one to mind him. But, my children, he had learned the true secret of making money; the true secret of how to get rich. This poor man, who had not a cent in the world, was making money all his life. Yes, and he was doing more than making it, he was laying it by safely in God's good bank in Heaven, and when he died he found it all there quite safe. He is living on his income now—living for all eternity on the riches he laid up in Heaven.

Which do you wish to be like? You can make your choice now; it is not even necessary for you to be a beggar in this world in order to be rich in Heaven; it is only necessary that you should not love the riches or pleasures of this world more than God; that you should try even when you are earning money by your honest labor to do it for God, to make a good resolution to do it because it is God's will, and not merely for the sake of having money to spend even on good and necessary objects.

My children, let us all pray to God very often that we may not love the world nor the things of the world, for the world will pass away, and it is not worth our while to set our affections on it.

CHAPTER III.

THE HONOR OF BEING SERVANTS.

WE often hear people say in a tone of contempt, "Oh she is only a servant!" We often hear girls say, "Oh what can I do? I'm only a poor servant." My children, this is the world's idea, this is the world's opinion, but it is not what God says, it is not what the holy Angels say.

The Angels are servants, they are God's servants, for they are all day long doing His holy will. Let us think of this for a little while, that we may see what a great honor it is to be a servant.

My children, our Lord Jesus Christ was a servant. He, the very King of kings, and the very Lord of lords—He took on Him the very form of a servant for our sake; how then can any one consider it a degradation to be a servant?

Listen to the words of the Holy Apostle:

For let this mind be in you which was in Christ Jesus,

Who, being in the form of God, thought it not robbery to be equal with God:

But emptied himself, taking the form of a servant, being made in the likeness of man and in habit found as a man. (Philip ii., 5–7.)

My children, see what our Lord Jesus Christ did to atone for our pride, and to teach us humility. He knew how hard it was for us to humble ourselves. He knew how we all love the honors of this poor world, how we would like to be looked up to and thought a great deal about, and how we dread humiliation or contempt. And He knew also that we would learn best by example, so He gave us Himself the example.

The world gives us the example of pride; our dear Saviour Jesus Christ gives us the example of humility. My children, we must take our choice, we must follow the example which the world gives us of pride, or the example which Jesus gives us of humility.

He Himself tells us that humility was the very special lesson which he came to teach us. "*Learn of me,*" He says, "*because I am meek and humble of heart, and you shall find rest to your souls.*" (St. Matthew.) And again:

Blessed are the poor in spirit, for theirs is the kingdom of Heaven.

Blessed are the meek, for they shall possess the land. (St. Matthew, v., 3–4.)

This is what God says. But the world does not say so. The world thinks that the rich and the mighty are blessed, that the great and the grand are blessed.

But even the world will admit that it is an honor to serve a great man. The world has its own ideas of greatness, and though its ideas are wrong very often, yet we may learn something from it. People do not think it any dishonor or humiliation to be the servant of a King or an Emperor. It is wonderful how low people will stoop when they want to get into the favor of some distinguished person.

But who is so great as God? and if it is an honor to serve a person of high rank or great fame, how great an honor must it not be to serve God Himself!

YOUNG CATHOLIC WOMEN. 51

We know, too, that the object of those who serve the rich or the great is that they may get rewarded for their service, and we know also that great people reward those who serve them in proportion to what they do. If you are able to render some very important service to a rich man he will pay you well for it, unless he is very mean. If you are able to serve a great Prince, or King, he will bestow rank on you as well as money, and may place you in what the world calls a very high position.

But how long will rank last? and how long will the money last? It will last just till you die. No longer, not another hour.

Perhaps after a person receives these rewards for his service, he might live ten or twenty, or thirty years; but then he dies, and there is an end of it. Eternity will last for ten or twenty or thirty thousand years, and even so many more that we cannot even attempt to count them. And what will he have to show for his service then? why just nothing—nothing.

My children, let us be wise. Let us be the servants of the good, good God, who will reward us for ever and ever, and who will give us true riches and true rank, not for ten years or for twenty years, but for ever and for ever.

Now you will see what an honor it is to be a servant. It is the greatest honor we can possibly have to be the servants of Our Lord Jesus Christ. But besides this great honor, which every good Christian may have, I wish to show to those who may read this little book, and who are obliged to be the servants of an earthly master, how great an honor they have.

My children, you who are servants and who are obliged to do the work of servants for others, whether you do it by laboring for them in your own homes, or in the families of your employers, you should think yourself very happy, for many saints have lived just this very kind of life, and our Lord Jesus lived and worked as the servant of others—and think what an honor it is to be like Him.

Perhaps you have said to yourself sometimes, "Oh, I wish I was like my mistress; she has nothing to do all day but amuse herself; she has fine clothes and plenty of the best of food, and no care or trouble to get it." Suppose that all this is true; your mistress may not be any richer than you are. The poor are very often inclined to think that the rich have no troubles, that those who have money can never want anything else. But this is a very great mistake. Money will not keep away death, or sickness, or family troubles; and the rich must die, and suffer just as much as the poor. The only true riches, because the long riches, which will last for ever, are the riches which we lay up in Heaven, and the poor servant has quite as many opportunities of laying up this treasure as the rich mistress.

There will no doubt be many people in Heaven who were rich on earth. Who loved God more than their money, and who used their money for God's glory more than for their own pleasure. But our Lord has told us Himself that there is great danger for rich people, and that it is hard for them to get through this world and the next to Heaven; and since God, who is the very truth Himself, and who knows all our hearts and thoughts, has said this, do you not think you are better off to be poor?

Besides, you have the honor to be like our Lord Jesus Christ. For the future, instead of saying, "Oh, how I wish I was like that rich lady, and had plenty of money, to do what I like with!" say, "Oh, how I should thank God that I am poor, like my Lord Jesus Christ; that I have the honor of being obliged to serve others, like my Lord Jesus Christ!"

In the Holy House of Nazareth, where our Blessed Saviour lived for so many years, with Mary and Joseph, He served His blessed Mother, and His foster father, St. Joseph. You may be sure that our Lord did all the hard work in that Holy House, as soon as He was able.

You may be sure that He cleaned the rooms, and brought the water, and helped to cook the food. Our Lady and St. Joseph were too poor to keep servants. My children, if the poor only knew how they might sanctify all their labor by uniting it to the labor of Jesus, how happy they would be, and how rich they would be.

The great thing is the intention; you must wish to unite your labor to the labor of Jesus, and you can do this every morning by saying the little verse at page 35 of this book. You need not be thinking about it all day, though it would be very well if you gave it a thought sometimes; but you should certainly make this offering, or some offering like it, every morning. By doing this you engage yourself, as it were, in the service of your Heavenly Master. You engage yourself with Him to work for Him all day long. You will see, when you go to Heaven, how richly He will pay you.

You will lay up treasures for yourself that will make you rich to all Eternity; and, besides, you will really get on better in this world. People who commit sin never prosper. They may get on well for a while. They may lay by a great deal of money, and have fine dresses, and grand carriages, and all the pomp and pride of this life, but in the end some great downfall comes, their sins are sure to find them out, something they have never expected will happen, and all that they have so carefully laid up is taken from them; and then see how miserable they are! They have no pleasure in this world, and they have no hope in the next world; even those who once praised them will turn against them, and those who envied them will laugh at them—and this is the end. Yes, my children, this is the end in this world, and a very miserable end; but what is the end in the next—in the world which will last forever and forever? They have never thought about it—they have never prepared for it; but they must go there, and they can take nothing with them—surely these poor people are indeed to be pitied!

Let us then learn to be the faithful servants of our Lord Jesus Christ. No matter who we serve in this world—no matter whether we are rich or poor, let us be the servants of our dear Lord. Let us think, first of all, of what will please Him, and last of all, of what will please ourselves. And we should remember, for our help and comfort, that we may be the servants of Jesus in every position in life. If it was our duty to sweep the streets, we could still do that for our Lord Jesus Christ, and be rewarded by Him hereafter.

Let us begin from this very day, and learn to try with our whole hearts to love our dear Lord and Saviour, and to do everything we can to please Him.

CHAPTER IV.

SOME ADVICE ABOUT DIFFERENT DUTIES WHICH WE MAY HAVE TO DO.

You know, I am sure, that every one has a guardian Angel. A bright, beautiful spirit has been appointed by God to take care of each human soul, and to watch it from the moment of its creation until the moment of its death.

Some of the holy guardian angels are employed in minding kings and queens; some are employed in minding ladies and gentlemen; and some are employed in minding poor beggars. Yes, even the unhappy people who are in prison for their crimes have guardian angels, who are watching them—watching to see if they will repent—watching to see if they will be sorry for having offended the good, good God.

The drunkard who goes reeling down the streets has a guardian angel. And, my child, you, too, have a guardian angel. Do you ever think about him, or pray to him?

He is standing beside you NOW—quite close to you. He is looking at you, he is watching every good thought; and then how pleased he is when you say that you will try to follow *good advice*, and to make yourself every day more holy.

The guardian angels do not choose their own work; God chooses it for them. I want you to think about this. We all like to choose our own employments; we all have different tastes and inclinations; but though there is no sin in this, we must remember that it is sometimes a sin, or rather, that we may commit sin by wanting to follow our own inclinations. This is called self will. It is a very dangerous temptation; and people who cannot do what they wish often commit a great deal of imperfection, by complaining that they cannot have their own way, and perhaps by trying to get it.

We must try to be like the holy guardian angels. My children, your good angel is as well content to mind and take care of you as if you were the greatest person in the world. The angel guardian of a poor sinner is quite as content to mind him as if he were a great saint.

And why is this? It is because the holy angels never wish to choose for themselves, and never desire to do anything except what God wishes.

We must try to be like the angels. It is not easy for us, because we are poor, weak, sinful creatures, and our human wills and inclinations are more inclined to do wrong than to do right, but we must remember that God's good grace is *never* wanting to us; that God will always help us if we will only ask Him.

A girl who has to mind little children will say: "Oh, how I hate those troublesome children! I wish I had something else to do." A girl who is cook will say: "Dear, dear, *my* work is never done, and the mistress sees so much company, and no one has any consideration for me." The girl who does sewing will say: "I wish I was in a place where I could run about, and not be all day at this machine." A girl who has to attend others will say: "Well, I am never off my legs, I wish I could sit still for an hour."

The truth is, people are very seldom really content with their state in life. And this discontent is both wrong and foolish. It is wrong because God has placed us all in different positions in the world, and we ought to be quite content with His holy will, and to desire only to be what, and to be where He wishes us to be. It is foolish because all the grumbling in the world won't make any change for us, and it will only make us unhappy, and make those about us unhappy if we give way to it.

God has put everything in the world in the place He wishes it to be. Each star has its own place in the sky, and if it went out of its place, what confusion would be caused. We do not know why one person is born rich and another poor; why one person is born to do one kind of work, and another person to do another kind of work, but God knows, and as all that he does is wisest and best, we ought not only to be content, but even to be thankful. We shall perhaps know about these things in Heaven, and then we shall see what we must here take on trust.

It sometimes happens that our situations or employments seem to come to us by what we call accident. A girl is offered a place and she takes it, but these things are not accidents.

My children, our blessed Lord Himself has told us that the very hairs of our heads are numbered; that not even one little bird can fall to the ground without His knowledge and permission, and how much more will He not, and does He not direct everything that concerns us.

It is true, that we have a free will, which the birds and stars have not; we have a choice. If a situation is offered to a girl, she can take it or refuse it. If she takes it for good intentions, she may be sure that she is doing God's will, and she ought to be content and happy. But there are some girls, unhappily, who do not think about God's will; who only think of themselves; who will refuse a situation with a good Catholic family, and take one with Protestants, who they know will try to pervert them from their faith, or try to prevent them from attending to their religious duties, just because they expect to get more money, or to have less work to do. This is not doing God's holy will, like the blessed guardian Angels.

It is remarkable how many directions are given in the Bible to servants. When our blessed Lord came to preach the gospel, it was the poor who listened to Him most willingly, and the poor who followed Him most faithfully. And when the Apostles went to preach, it was just the same.

The Apostle St. Paul says to servants that they should be obedient to their masters as to Christ. My children, think of this:

"*Not serving to the eye, as it were pleasing men, but, as the servants of Christ, doing the will of God from the heart: not serving to the eye.*"—(Ephesians vi., 6.)

Does it not sometimes happen that girls in service, or those who are in any way employed to work for others, will say: "Oh, it is no matter how I do that; no one will see it, no one will be the wiser!"

My children, this is serving to the eye, and doing the very thing which God tells you not to do. You are to do your work "from the heart." You know how you work when your heart is in your work; well, you should always work that way, not for any earthly motive, but for our Lord Jesus Christ, because you are to work as the "servant of Christ."

But there is one more advice:

"With a good will serving, as to the Lord, and not to man."—(Eph. vi., 7.)

Not grudgingly or impatiently, by thinking it hard; that would not be working with a good will. Your work may indeed be hard and troublesome; you may often feel very tired and weary. There is no harm in this, you will only have all the more merit for it if you can bear it patiently; but for all this, you must try and serve with a good will.

People do not think much of labor or fatigue when they are working for themselves; it is only when they are working for others that they complain. It is true, indeed, that there are some masters and mistresses who have very little thought for their servants, and who try to make them do more work than they are really able to do; now if you should happen to be with those who required you to do more than you thought you could bear, it would not be necessary or even right for you to stay in such a place. All that you are obliged to do, is to try and do all reasonable work as well as you can, and from the pure motive of doing it to please God. When you have done your best, if those whom you serve are not satisfied, you are not to be troubled. There is a great Master over them and over you, and if He is pleased, that is enough.

ADVICE ABOUT MINDING CHILDREN.

You, who have charge of children, have a most holy and blessed duty confided to you, and one for which you must certainly give an account at the great Day of Judgment. If I were to write all that I wish to write about the different duties of the different states of life and occupations, I should write a very large book, which I cannot do at present. But the duty of minding children is so important that I must say all I can:

There are very few people who have not charge of children at some time or other of their lives. At home, the older girls should take care of the younger ones; at school the elder girls should do what they can to help them; in service there are many whose whole time is dedicated to children, and nearly every servant some time or other has to do with them, and there are very many who will read this book, who may have children of their own; or will one day, please God, be married and have the care of a family. How important it is that people should learn how to take proper care of little children.

The holy Angels will reward those who are kind and good to those poor little helpless ones.

Those who have charge of children should make the sign of the cross on them, and say some short prayer for them every day, night and morning, until the child is old enough to say prayers for itself.

It is dreadful to think how some people who call themselves good Catholics, will let their children grow to be quite big without teaching them their prayers.

Remember this is a duty you cannot commence too soon. When the dear little one begins to take notice, it will see that you look serious, but not cross, for a few minutes every night and morning, and that you try to fold its little hands and say to yourself some prayers for it; by-and-by, when it begins to speak, you can teach it to say JESUS AND MARY. Then you can teach it to say some very short prayer, and so lead it on by degrees.

You must give the child good example; you will be surprised at this; you will say, "What matter what I do or say before a little child!" My children, it is a great deal of matter. One day you will be telling every one how clever the child is, and how it notices everything, and how smart it is; and the next day you will say, "Oh, never mind; the child cannot know." Which is right?

Believe me, that very, very young children know and notice, and that they will remember things that have happened even before they can speak plain.

Think how cruel and wicked it is to give a child bad example. When you do, you are teaching it to please the devil. Whenever you say bad words, or get into a passion, or talk about things that children should never hear, you are just acting as if you threw mud and dirt on a beautiful white satin dress.

The little child's soul is white and pure, and you are trying to make it dark and ugly.

I have even known people who have been so wicked as to teach little children to say bad words for mere amusement; they think it is so funny to hear a child curse and swear, and say, "What harm? sure, the child does not mean it—it does not know what it is saying!"

The poor child certainly does not know it; but the person who teaches her knows, and I promise you she will not laugh about it at the Day of Judgment. Again: nurses, and even parents, will teach children tricks, just as they would teach a monkey or dog; and perhaps in a year or two they will punish the child for doing the very things they taught it to do themselves. Do you know what our Lord said Himself about little children, when He was on earth? He said:

"*He that shall scandalize one of these*

little ones that believe in me, it were better for him that a millstone should be hanged about his neck, and that he should be drowned in the depths of the sea."—(St. Matt. xviii., 6).

And yet how little people think of the sin of giving scandal to children—of giving them bad example, and how much worse is it to teach them evil!

You have all heard of St. Aloysius, the holy Jesuit, who died so young. Well, when he was a little child he was taught some bad words by some soldiers, and though it was not his fault, and though he had not committed the least sin, or even imperfection, by repeating these words, still he grieved about it all his life, as we should grieve, and perhaps a great deal more than we ever grieved for a mortal sin.

ADVICE TO

My children, above all things take the very tenderest care of Christ's little ones. Bear with them, and comfort them in their little troubles and sickness; nurse them tenderly, as Mary nursed the Infant Jesus; think often of her example. Be gentle to them; be loving to them. If they do wrong, as children will do wrong, do not fly in a passion with them, but speak to them gently and nicely, and if it is necessary, punish them, but never punish a child in anger. Do not revenge on them your own feeling of annoyance at what they have done.

You should also be very careful never to say to children, "Don't tell your mamma so and so." You may be sure if there is anything that you do not wish your mistress to know, that it is wrong; and even if it were no harm—only a thing you did not wish known—you do the poor child a great injury, for you are teaching it to be deceitful.

ADVICE ABOUT DOMESTIC SERVICE.

A domestic servant has a great deal in her power; she may help to make her mistress's house very happy, or very uncomfortable. One of the first things that a domestic servant should study, is a habit of order and cleanliness. Some servants will do twice as much work as others; not because they are stronger or more willing, but because they have a better method—they do every duty in regular order; and unless they are called away, and cannot help it, they finish one duty well and carefully before they begin another.

There is a great deal more in method or regularity than people think. A place for everything, and everything in its proper place; and a time for everything, and everything in its time, are golden rules for every one. These are wise rules, both in a spiritual and a temporal point of view. Our Blessed Lord has told us to secure the Kingdom of Heaven *first*—that is, to give the first place, in our plans and objects and intentions, to Heaven, and all the rest will be sure to come right after.

Let us see how this rule works for domestic servants.

CHAPTER V.

THE SAME SUBJECT CONTINUED.

A GIRL who has a place for everything, and a time for everything, has a place and a time for her prayers. My children, I fear there are many people who never think of prayer.

Let us ask ourselves, first, what is prayer? and then, when we have learned what it is, and the great necessity and value of it, we may be more anxious about it.

What is Prayer?

Prayer is asking God for what we want.

God is our Father. He has Himself taught us to call Him Father, and say, when we speak to Him, "Our Father." Now let us think what a good father is. A good father is one who loves his children, and will be most anxious to do everything he possibly can for them. But the very best and kindest father in the world cannot always do what he wishes for his children. He has not the power. If he is poor he cannot make them rich. If he is hungry he cannot give them bread. If he is ignorant he cannot give them wisdom.

But our great and good Father, God, is rich, and wise, and all-powerful, and He can give us everything we ask Him for. But you will say, perhaps, that you have asked Him for many things that He has not given you.

My children, we must remember that God is a *good* Father, and that He is a *wise* Father; that no one but God can know what is really good for us, and that we are like poor foolish children, who ask for things that are very bad for us; and surely we would not wish God to give us what would be bad for us.

We say to God, " Give us this day our daily bread." My children, we often ask God for things that would be far worse for us than poisons. And why? Because poison would only kill our bodies; but we sometimes ask God for things which would kill our souls if He gave them to us.

Let us be quite sure that God hears every prayer we offer, and let us be quite sure that God answers it.

If a little child asked you for a knife would you give it to her? Certainly not.

But the child might think you very unkind and very cross, not to give her the knife. But you would not mind—you would say to yourself, "Poor little thing; she will know better when she gets older." She is too young to know that the knife would only cut her—you would not mind how much she cried.

My children, we often cry for things which would do us far more harm than the knife would do the child, but the good God will not give them to us. He loves us too much. But He will give us something else instead. We may be quite sure, when God refuses to give us anything that we have asked for, that He gives us in place of it something else that is really good for us.

Well, then, a good girl begins in the morning by prayer. When she is called in the morning, or when she knows it is time to get up and begin the day's work, she does not turn about and stretch herself, and say, "Oh, I am so cold!" or, "Oh, I am so tired!" or, "Oh, I am so sleepy!" or, "Oh, I am so hot!" or, "I am sure I may as well stay in bed a little, it cannot make any difference in the end!"

My children, this waiting a little to get up—for whatever reason—may make a difference to you, and a very great difference a hundred thousand years hence; nay, if I said a hundred hundred thousand years hence, it would be very short of the truth.

And why? Because, at the last great Day we shall be rewarded for every action of our lives; and that reward will last, and will be of benefit to us forever and forever.

My children, you would have no difficulty in rising very quickly and very early every morning of your life, whether you were tired or rested, or whether it was hot or cold, if you were sure of getting some great temporal benefit.

But, unfortunately, we think so little of ETERNITY—so little of the great, and wonderful, and everlasting riches which God has in store for us in the other world, and which *are so certain.*

If you delay—from whatever cause—in the morning, you do yourself a serious injury, because through your fault you lose the time which you ought to have given to prayer.

My children, you will never know in this world the importance of prayer—you will never know what you have lost when you have neglected prayer; and the worst of it is, that when you do know, it will be too late to remedy your error.

Morning is the time and place for prayer. Take care, then, that you pray at the right time and place; and if you do, you may be sure that everything else will go on well.

If you set at your work in the morning without taking any food, and worked on all day without food, you would feel quite faint and ill towards the evening. The harder you worked the worse you would be; and if you tried to work without food for several days you would probably die of starvation.

Your poor soul wants food quite as much, and even more than your body. The food that your soul wants is the grace of God, and you must ask Him for that every day.

"*Give us this day our daily bread,*" means give us this day the food that will support our souls, and make them strong and vigorous, as well as the food which will support our bodies. Do not let your soul starve. Ask and you shall have; for God will never refuse you what is for your eternal welfare.

Say your prayers fervently. Do not try to do two things at once; it will not answer, either in a temporal or a spiritual way. You know very well that you cannot do two things at once, and do both well. Some people kneel down to say their prayers, and all the time that they are saying the words they are thinking of something else. They are wondering will it be a fine day, or will some piece of work be done before evening; or they are thinking of what some one said yesterday, or if some one will do or say something to-day.

My children, this is very wrong. If you spoil or injure a piece of work that you are doing for this world it is a pity; but after all, the consequences are only temporal; but if you spoil or injure a work that you are doing for the next world, the consequences will be *Eternal.*

Say, now, and make a good resolution about your morning prayers. Begin the day well, and you will be sure to end it happily. Spend a few minutes, before you leave the room where you sleep, in saying your prayers fervently and earnestly, in asking God with your whole heart to give you grace to spend the day well, and to lay up treasures of Heaven. Say:

> My Lord, I offer Thee this day
> All I shall do, or think, or say—
> Uniting it with what was done
> On earth by Jesus Christ, Thy Son.

Then ask God to keep you from your predominate sin that day, whatever it may be. If you are passionate, say:

"My God, help me to keep my temper to-day, however I may be provoked."

If you are proud, say:

"My God, help me to be humble to-day, however I may be tempted to be proud."

If you are slothful, say:

"My God, help me to work well and faithfully to-day, and to overcome my natural indolence."

If you are fond of eating or drinking, say:

"My God, help me to overcome my love of eating and drinking to-day."

The girl who says her prayers well in the morning, will go down to her work as gay as a lark, She will work well because she is working for God; she will work cheerfully, because her mind will be at rest; she will be so happy herself that she will make every one else happy. You will hear her singing at her work some of the nice songs she learned at the Convent school, or some of the holy hymns she has learned at her parish church.

People will say, "What a nice, bright-looking girl!" Dear children, God is the source of all joy, of all happiness. The angels are always bright and happy, the devils are always miserable and wretched. Good people have their troubles; the good girl, who says her prayers regularly, who prays to the saints regularly, will have her troubles as well as the bold girl, but depend upon it, her mind will still be happy.

There may be tears in her eyes for death of her friends, or for her own troubles or sickness, but there will be peace in her heart.

Her work will be well done, because she will give her whole mind to it; she will have a regular order and method in it, and she will try to do everything as well as she possibly can.

Look at the girl who got up late, who gave way to her indolence, and then said she had not time to say her prayers.

She gets up cross, because she knows very well she has done wrong, and so she is put out of temper. A nice beginning for the day! She is angry with herself, but she has not the honesty to blame herself, and so she blames every one else.

Her clothes are put on "any how," and she looks for all the world as if she had slept in them. She does not wash herself, for she says she "has not time" for that either, and so she feels very uncomfortable, and no wonder, for cleanliness is next to godliness, and after saying your prayers, there is nothing brightens a girl up, and improves her temper and appearance, like a good wash.

She goes down stairs, ready to quarrel with every one. The poor cat is in her way, or comes to meet her with a pleasant purr; but she gives it a kick, and ten to one in so doing she falls over a stool or a sauce-pan and hurts herself—her temper gets worse.

Then the fire won't light; it is all the fault of the wood. She knocks it about as she knocked the cat, and of course, the fire does not get hot any sooner. The mistress comes down and calls for breakfast, or the master for hot water. Hot water! if they came near her she would give them plenty. She gives an angry answer, and in her hurry and vexation oversets everything, and then all has to be done over again.

Her mistress is very angry, and no wonder. Her master has his business to mind, and he cannot afford to be late for it, or the poor children in the nursery are crying for their breakfast, and the mistress knows that they ought not to be kept waiting. Then there are angry words, and the girl sits down and has a "good cry," and thinks her mistress very unreasonable, and wastes as much time as would have allowed her to have said her prayers well and steadily, and blames the poor cat, and the stools, and the saucepans, and the mistress, and every one—except herself.

My children, you must surely have known people who have just acted in that way, and I am sure you do not wish to be like them. If you do not, take care to do everything in its right time, and to keep everything in its right place, and above all, to begin the day well.

CHAPTER VI.

ADVICE ABOUT HONESTY.

HONESTY is the best policy. So says the old proverb, and if you will think about it, you will find that the old proverb is true. But we must not think of honesty as the best policy only for this world, though it certainly is the best; we must think about honesty as being the most pleasing to God.

I am afraid there are very many who have very confused or indistinct ideas about honesty. Sometimes this is because they are not really well instructed, and sometimes, I am afraid, I ought to say very often, it is because they do not choose to be strictly honest, and so they say to themselves, that certain things are "no harm."

My children, I have spoken to you before about the *great harm* by doing things which you excuse to yourself by saying, "it is no harm," but now I have to speak of some very serious matters.

It often happens, indeed it generally happens, that a master or mistress are obliged to trust a great deal to their servants. I have already told you what a great and holy task it is to have the care of children, and what an account those who have charge of them must give to God.

But you may be, and in many cases you must be, trusted with the property of others, and you ought to ask yourself very often, and very seriously, how do you fulfill your duty? You may fail in honesty in two ways.

First, you may fail in honesty by not taking care of the goods confided to your charge, and this is bad enough.

Second, you may fail in honesty by stealing what you have charge of, and this is a great deal worse.

A cook has many and great temptations in this way. If she is careless, she may spoil as much food in a day as would serve for two days. If she is living in a large family, where there are a great many servants, she may waste a very great deal of food, and what is this but actually robbing her employers?

She would be very sorry indeed to put her hand into her mistress's pocket and take out a dollar. She would, let us hope, think it very wrong; but she will not trouble herself for a second about spoiling a dollar's worth, no nor twenty dollars' worth of good food. Now consider this a little. Suppose you let twenty dollars worth of food spoil in hot weather from want of sufficient care, which you might easily have saved. Your master must buy twenty dollars' worth more of food, and is not this just taking the money from him?

There are many ways of wasting food, and I have not time to go into the subject here, but I am quite sure every one who reads this, and has charge of cooking for a family, will know very well what I mean.

Let me beg of you, for your poor soul's sake, if you have been careless about this, to begin now to be very careful.

It is easy to say, "it is only an accident," to put things on the cat, or on the weather, or a fellow servant; but excuses won't do in the other world, and careless servants can't expect the reward that God will give hereafter to those who have served their masters faithfully for His sake.

But what shall I say of those who actually steal; who take inferior articles, or articles that are under weight from the stores, and then take a bribe from the person they were buying from. They are just robbing their employers. They need not give their conduct any nice name, or excuse themselves by talking about their "perquisites," or saying that other people "do the same."

Do you suppose that it will make you suffer less in the other world if other people are punished with you? It is a most common and a most fatal deceit when people excuse themselves for doing wrong by saying that "other people" do wrong also. What difference will it make to you? Is a sin less a sin because some one else commits it.

My children, if every one in the world committed sins of thought, or any other sin, that would not be the very best excuse for you. Remember; and as you love your poor soul, never, never forget that God will judge YOU for what you do, and not for what other people do.

Do you think you will dare to say to God, at the Day of Judgment, "I stole because other people stole;" or, "I was no worse than any fellow-servant."

Would you dare to say this to any earthly judge? and if you did say it, do you think he would listen to such an excuse?

And what shall I say of those who are so dishonest as to steal money, and jewels, and dress? A girl finds some money, and takes no trouble to discover the owner, and she keeps it for herself. A girl sees a purse lying on her master's table, and perhaps she thinks she will never be suspected, and she takes it. She sees a ring and a brooch, and she says, "No one will know," and she takes it. Poor girl, poor girl! she thinks to make herself happy by having this money, or this dress, or these pieces of finery; but she is miserable—miserable.

Sometimes she thinks she will restore it, but the devil won't let her; he tries every effort to keep her from carrying out her intention—from confessing her fault.

She says, "If I tell, what will people think of me?" but she never says, "What will God think of me?"

Better a thousand times for you to confess your fault, and endure any punishment in this world, than to suffer punishment hereafter—perhaps even to lose your soul in the world to come.

Sin never makes any one happy. When a person steals, she steals because she thinks it will make her happy to have what she has wished for; but she soon finds her mistake. If she steals money, she would like to spend it on dress; but she is afraid, for she knows people will wonder how she got the money to buy such good clothes. If she has stolen jewels she does not wear them, and she is almost afraid to keep them.

But the devil has succeeded, and he

only laughs at her folly, as he will laugh at her in Hell if he can tempt her to commit sin after sin, until he gets her there.

My children, it is easy to resist temptation in the beginning if you ask the help of God's holy grace; but if you do not resist in the beginning you will find it harder and harder every day.

Temptation is like a fire; at first we see only a little spark, and it is easy to put it out; but if it is not put out at once, it gets by-and-by to be a great blaze, and then, indeed, it is hard to put it down; but I shall say more of this in the next chapter.

CHAPTER VII.

ADVICE ABOUT TEMPTATIONS.

As long as we live in this world we shall be subject to temptations. Even the very holiest people are tempted, for the devil goes about—or rather, a great many devils go about trying to make us commit sin.

It is our own fault if they succeed in their wicked purpose. God has given us the Holy Sacraments, and His Holy grace to enable us to overcome every evil; and if we do not choose to use the help which God has given us we have no one to blame but ourselves.

My children, it is of the greatest possible importance that we should learn how to resist temptations. I am going to say a few words to you about this, and I hope you will read this over carefully and often.

There is no sin in being tempted. The saints were tempted; our blessed Lord was tempted. The sin is not in the temptation, which we cannot help, but in the yielding to the temptation, which we can help.

Every one is not tempted the same way. The devil knows very well the different inclinations and passions of each person, and he suits his temptations to those inclinations or passions. He sees a girl who is fond of dress and finery, and he tries to tempt her to get dress and finery by dishonest ways. He sees a girl who is, perhaps, very good and obedient to her parents, and he tempts her to steal a few dollars to help them, and tries even to make her think it no harm.

Listen, my children: Beware of that " no harm." Yes; I know I have said it before, and you are tired of hearing it; but never mind, if often telling you makes you think more about it, and so keeps you from committing sin—that is all I want.

The devil does not care the very least whether he tempts you by bad motives or good ones. It is indeed a good motive to help your parents—a most holy motive, and one that God approves, and from which thousands of Irish girls act; but the devil does not like to see them so generous and charitable; he knows what treasures they have laid up for themselves in God's Bank in Heaven—he wants to rob them, and prevent them from laying up any more; and he tries to make them take something, perhaps only some very little thing, to which they have no right—something which is not their own—all out of a wrong idea of duty to their parents; sometimes, even, he will make them take something to give to help a convent, or for a fair that is being held for some good object.

He will say to a girl, in her mind, "See, such a girl has given more than you; the priest will think more of her;" and he will tempt you by pride—by making you feel quite vexed that any one should do more than you do. This is a dreadful temptation. In the first place, when you give anything in charity, you should do it for the love of God. A person might give away his whole fortune to the poor, and be no better for it in the next world. The best action in the world becomes worthless if it is done from a bad motive. Dear children, try to have a good motive in everything you do. It is not difficult. There is only one really good motive, and that is the love of God.

If you were to give every dollar you ever earned to build churches or help convents, it would be of little use unless you did it for the love of God. And the more freely you do it for the love of God, the more reward you will have.

I will explain this because I am very anxious indeed that you should understand it.

Suppose you were in great want of money to buy food—that you were starving—and that some friend came and gave you some money; you would be very grateful to her, and so you ought. But suppose you heard soon after that she had been boasting to every one of what she had done—telling all the neighbors, and trying to get praise for it—would you think the same of her? I am sure you would not.

You would say, "Well, I am sure I shall always be obliged to her for her kindness, but I see now it was not all for me she did it; I see she wanted to be thought very charitable, and to be praised for it." And you would be just that much less obliged to her.

Now, my children, when you give money to the poor, or to your parents, or to the church, you do it, I am sure, first for the love of God—and many of you, I hope, do it entirely for the love of God—

but sometimes you are a little proud of it, and proud that you gave more than others did, and you like to hear it talked about by your friends. Well, God will reward you in Heaven for it, as far as you did it for Him; but you will not get as much as you might have gotten if you had not wanted to be praised for it. You see, we cannot have our reward both in this world and the next. When we are praised for anything here, or rather, when we wish to be praised, for we cannot help people praising us, it is not their doing so which injures us, but our wishing them to do so; then we just lose so much of our reward in the other world, and when we think that this reward will be lost forever and ever, it is surely worth our while to take great pains to secure it.

The way in which people generally fall

is by listening to temptations, by not turning their back on the devil *at once*. It is so important that you should learn to do this, that I cannot say too much about it.

When a thought comes into your mind to do anything which you know to be wrong, you should turn from it at once and say a short prayer to God to help you. But listen, my children, there are some people who say a prayer with their lips, while all the time they are keeping the temptations in their minds. They have one eye on the temptation—they are looking at the article of dress, or the gold, or whatever it may be that they are tempted to steal, and do you think that is resisting temptation properly? Indeed it is not.

You must help yourself, and then God will help you. The longer you look at what tempts you, the more likely you are to take it. The longer you keep an evil thought in your heart, the sooner you will consent to it. If you saw a lion coming down the street, would you wait to see whether it would kill you? You would not; no, indeed! you would take to your heels, and a fine race you would make of it, and put as many blocks as you could between you and danger. And this is what you must do when you are tempted.

Remember that almighty God has given you free will. People say, "Oh, I could not help it!" when they do wrong; but that is a lie. It would be of very little use to you to say that at the day of Judgment. You can help it. If we could not help doing wrong it would be unjust for God to punish us for it. If a child was to steal some sugar and then say, "I could not help it!" would you believe the child?

There is another thing, also, you must remember about temptation, which is, that you cannot resist it without the help of God's grace. You must ask for this grace. God is more willing to give it than you are to ask for it. If God were to give us grace without our asking, so as to compel us to be good, then we would have no merit. He gives us the necessary grace to enable us to be saved; but we must ask for it.

Whenever you are tempted, think of this; if you think of it often it will come easily to your mind when the temptation comes.

We must always be ready for temptation, because we do not know the moment it may come. Our life is one long warfare with the devil and our own evil inclinations. The devil wants to get us down to Hell, that he may have us there to torment us forever; God and the holy Angels invite us to Heaven.

We must make our choice; there is no place between. All day long the choice is open to us. When we are tempted, the devil is trying to make us choose Hell, for if he can get us to commit a mortal sin, we are in his power; he can take us off to Hell if we die in mortal sin. God and the holy Angels and holy Mary are inviting us up to Heaven.

My children, turn your back on the devil, and get away from him as fast as you can. The very moment you are tempted say a short prayer—say the "Hail Mary," or, "Oh God, come to my assistance, oh God, make haste to help me!" but when

God sends help, you must use it; you must turn away from the temptation, and if it is an evil thought, if it returns again and again, pray again and again, and you will be sure to conquer.

CHAPTER VIII.

ADVICE ABOUT PRAYER AND THE SACRAMENTS.

My children, we cannot live without prayer, that is, our souls cannot live. It is wonderful how anxious people are about the life of their bodies: about this poor life which must end so soon. When God says "you must die," no one in the world can keep you. You must go, and nothing in the world can prevent it. We must all die, and this a thing which it is very certain must be.

Death is indeed the only thing in the world of which we can be certain. We *must* die, and we do not know when that great and terrible event will happen. There is nothing which young people find so hard to realize as the certainty of death. They feel themselves full of life and vigor and high spirits, and they will not think of it. But this does not make their lives any longer. You must die! There is nothing uncertain about death except the time; it may be soon, it may not be for years; but as the event is so certain, and of such fearful importance, surely, surely, you cannot be too well prepared for it.

When you die your real life will begin, and it is for this life that you should incessantly prepare by prayer and the holy Sacraments of the Church. I intend now, with God's help, to say a few words about prayer and about the Sacraments:

You know that if you do not eat, you cannot live; your body will die. And my children, if you do not pray and use the Sacraments, your soul will die; and think, oh think what a dreadful thing the death of your soul would be! Think of what Hell is—think of what Heaven is, and remember, if you go to Hell when you die, you will have no one to blame but yourself. May God in His great and tender Mercy grant that no one who shall read this little book may ever see that place of torment.

ADVICE ABOUT PRAYER.

I have already said a good deal about the duty of saying your prayers every morning, and saying them well. Better say a few prayers with your whole heart and mind, than to spend an hour on your knees muttering over the words, and thinking of something else.

Remember, first—

To whom you are speaking.

Remember, second—

What you are speaking about.

You are speaking to the great God who has made Heaven and earth. To the almighty God who has created you, and who in one second of time could send you to Hell, where, alas! we all deserve to be for our sins.

You must speak to the good God with reverence, with attention, with respect.

If you were speaking to a King or Queen, or to any great man of this world, would you be thinking of something else all the time, or looking about you? If you did this, would you not deserve to be sent away at once from their presence?

Remember to whom you are speaking; that it is your own interest, your own good, your own benefit.

My children, if you went to some friends to ask them a good favor, and if you were all the time looking about, and asking for it as if you were saying a lesson you had learned off by heart, or if you did not care whether you had got it or not; what would the person think? He would think you did *not* care, and would say, "Well, I am sure she cannot want this favor, or she would ask it more earnestly!"

When we pray we are asking God for great favors, or we are thanking Him for the favors He has given us, and we must not dare to make a mock of prayer.

What I have said about prayer, refers to your night and morning prayers, to the prayers you say at Mass, and when you are preparing for Confession and for the holy Communion.

But besides our regular times of prayer there are times when we ought to say some special prayers. You know that there are times when we require more nourishment for our bodies than what we usually take; when we are tired—when our bodily strength is tired from hard work, we require more food. People are generally very careful about their bodily strength; they will get all the food they can to keep that up, but they do not think of their poor souls.

But my children, our souls need food as well as our bodies, and even more. You must have heard of the great famine in Ireland, when so many thousand people died. Well, there were many good, holy

Irish men, and women, and boys, and girls, who might have lived in this world, if they would have sold their souls for a bit of bread. But they would not. Oh no! They held the faith of St. Patrick too dear for that. The tempter said, "Go to the Protestant church, deny your religion and I will give you bread," but they said, "No!" and they died holy martyrs; they would not starve their souls; they bore the cruel pains of bodily starvation sooner than offend God.

They are not sorry for it now. They are where they can never feel hunger or thirst, or cold or heat. They are safe with God. And if we wish to be with them some day we must imitate their example. It may not be necessary for us to choose between dying of starvation in this world, and suffering eternal starvation in the next, but we are all obliged in some way or other to make a choice.

When temptation comes we must say, "I will," or "I will not;" and we must give our poor souls more food, the more they are tempted, even if we must deprive ourselves of our bodily food to do this.

We must feed our souls by prayer and the Sacraments. If you are in a situation where you have many temptations, and where you cannot get necessary time for prayer or hearing Mass, you must be willing to suffer in your earthly prospects for the good of your soul, and take any other place, where you may perhaps get less of this world's goods, but where you may be able to do more for the great Future.

Try, then, to acquire a spirit of prayer —to get a habit of asking almighty God for what you want, as a child would ask his mother.

But, my children, besides prayer we have the grace of the Sacraments. Can we ever thank Him enough for this great, great favor? You know that our holy church teaches us that there are seven Sacraments, each of these ordained by God Himself, for our help and comfort in our earthly pilgrimage.

The first of these Sacraments is Baptism. When you were a little child, before you were able to commit actual sin, you were taken to the church and baptized—you were made one of God's own children. How good it was of God to take you thus into His own family—to wipe away the stain of original sin from your poor soul, and to make it pure and white. How dreadful it is when those who have charge of little children try to soil their poor souls, and put ugly, dirty sin on them. God must be indeed very angry with those who do this terrible injustice.

By Baptism you are admitted into the church, and obtain a right to all the privileges of the holy church. Think how great a grace this is, and how you should thank God for it.

By the Sacrament of Confirmation you obtain strength to keep the promises which your god-parents made for you at your Baptism, and the special gifts of the Holy Ghost. The Sacrament of Confirmation is very important, and it should be prepared for with very great care.

The Holy Spirit of God is always ready to help us to do right; and even if we have not received this Sacrament with all the reverence and devotions which we ought, we can still pray for God's Holy Spirit, and pray to God's Holy Spirit every day of our lives. It is indeed very much to be desired that people should have greater love for, and devotion to, God, the Holy Ghost—that they should continually ask His help, for it is the will of God that we should thus obtain spiritual strength, to enable us to conquer our temptations.

And what should I say about the most Holy Sacrament of the Body and Blood of our Lord Jesus Christ? It would require the pen of an Angel to say what should be said; and it would require the love of an Angel to thank God as we should thank Him for this wonderful gift.

In all the other Sacraments God gives us some very special grace, but in this Sacrament He gives us HIMSELF.

My children, we can never know in

this world all that Jesus does for us in the most Holy Sacrament, because its effects are hidden. We do not see the grace which God gives us in this most Holy Sacrament, but it is none the less real—none the less certain. The great power and grace of this Sacrament is that it unites with God. We might have thought when Jesus died for us on the Cross, that He had done everything that could be done for us sinners; but His love for us is so great that He desired to do still more.

He was about to give Himself for us on the Cross. The greatest love that we can show to a friend, is to sacrifice our lives for him, and so Jesus gave His life for us. If Jesus had not done this, we must have gone to Hell when we died. We deserved this punishment for our sins, but Jesus suffered the cruel punishment of death on the Cross, through his great love, to save us.

But He wished to give Himself *to* us also. My children, think how He loves us. He comes Himself, in the most Holy Sacrament, into our poor hearts, to make us good and holy, and like Himself; and as He died on the Cross, to save us from Hell's fire, so He gives Himself to us in the most Holy Sacrament to make us fit for Heaven.

How earnestly we should try to prepare ourselves for the visit of the King of kings. How beautifully pure and white and clean we should make the poor house of our souls, and how we should thank Him for His great love.

The SACRAMENT OF PENANCE is the way appointed by God Himself to prepare us for His visit. Now, when visitors are expected in a family, every preparation is made to receive them with welcome— every room is cleaned up and made as beautiful as possible; the more people care for their friends, the more they will do to make a welcome for them. My children, we say, in our beautiful Irish tongue, "A hundred thousand welcomes!" when we are very, very glad to see any one. My child, my dear, dear child, how many hundred thousand welcomes ought we not to have for our Friend Jesus? Oh, my children, there never was a friend like Jesus! and yet what should we say of those who think very little about that friend?—who have a hundred thousand thousand welcomes for every one else, and only a cold one for Jesus? What will we say of those who will not take even the least trouble to prepare for His visit—

who think once or twice a year often enough to ask Him into the house of our souls.

But it will not be so with you. I am sure it is not so—only we must remember that however much we may love Jesus, we can never, never love Him enough; and so we should always try to love Him more.

The best way to show our love is by our actions. If a person says she loves you, and never comes to see you, or shows you any affection, you do not think much of her professions of friendship. There are some people, too, who will talk a great deal, but they will do very little. My children, talk won't take us to Heaven; we must pray, we must think, we must work, we must even suffer. There is an old saying, that where there is a will there is a way; many a girl says, "Oh, I have not time to go to Confession regularly!" My children, this is only an excuse; if it was to a party of pleasure she would find time, depend on it.

There are, however, certain cases in which persons may not be able to go to the Sacrament as often as they would wish, and if they are really hindered by duty and necessary business, it is not wrong, for they have the good intentions, and God will accept that.

You ought to go regularly to the one Confessor, and not be changing about, unless you cannot possibly help it. You ought to prepare quietly and steadily for your Confession first by examining your conscience, to see what you have done wrong, and by making acts of contrition for it. If you made a short examination of conscience every night, when you are going to bed, and saying your night prayers, as every good girl should do, you would not take long preparing for Confession.

You should make your Confession in as few words as possible, and tell your own sins, and not other people's. Some persons, when they go to Confession, will keep the priest twice as long as is necessary, because they talk too much. "I got angry with the mistress, but she provoked me, and she said——" and here follows a whole story of what she said, and what she did to make you angry. Why, the good priest would want to have the patience of a saint himself not to get angry with you.

Tell your own sins, and no one else's, and if you have anything else to say, or any advice to ask of the priest, ask it after your confession. After you have received absolution, say, "May I ask your advice, Father, about some business?" and then say what you want, but even then, don't keep the priest with a long story, but just say what you have to say. I think it very right and very wise of girls, and particularly girls in service, to ask the advice of the priest if they are inclined to leave their place, or if they are going to marry, or if they are in any difficulty, and I very earnestly recommend every girl who reads this book to ask the priest's advice whenever she is in the least difficulty.

After you have been to Confession, you should spend a short time thanking God for the great grace He has granted you.

My children, if we only thought how

much it cost our blessed Lord to purchase this grace for us, we should benefit more by it, for we should think more of it. He paid the price of His own most precious Blood, that our sins might be forgiven.

I should say more to you about this, but you will find instructions in your Prayer Book for preparing for the Sacraments, and I hope, please God, to write a Prayer Book for you before long.

CHAPTER IX.

ADVICE ON THE SAINTS—SACRAMENTS, (CONTINUED.)

The Sacrament of extreme Unction is, as you know, the last Sacrament which prepares us for that beautiful Heavenly country, where there is no more sorrow, or sickness, or death. My children, our lives ought to be one long preparation for that happy home, where God and the holy Angels are waiting for us. But we are so wrapped up in the business and the pleasures of this world, that we think very little indeed about the next.

There is something very awful, but at the same time very consoling, in the last Sacraments. How good God is to us! how infinitely, how wonderfully merciful! When we were little unconscious babes He received us into His holy Church, and made us His own children by the beautiful Sacrament of baptism, and now, when we are near our last end, He give us another beautiful Sacrament to prepare us for the passage to our Eternal home.

There are many people, I fear, who do not think of God's mercies as they should —who do not thank Him for them as they should; and then there are also some persons who are so wicked and so ungrateful as to presume on God's mercies; they say, "God is very merciful," and so they take no care to prepare themselves for death and judgment. Yes, my children, it is indeed true that God is very merciful, but it is also true that He is very just.

How miserable are those who thus deceive themselves. They will know, when it is too late, how truly merciful God is, for His justice is true mercy.

God is merciful to those who love Him, but when we disobey His commands all our lives, when we never think of Him, when we even excuse our sins by saying: "God is merciful, I will repent before I die!" then we must feel His justice. He is too just not to punish the sinner. He is too just to show the same justice to the wicked that He does to the good. You have your choice now. You can secure for yourself now, against your last hour, the mercy or the justice of God.

My children, in that hour of death, the

best and the holiest will need mercy ; take care that you secure it now!

You know when the priest administers to us the Sacrament of Extreme Unction, he anoints our hands, and feet, and eyes, and ears, and mouth with the holy oil, praying that God may wipe away the sins we have committed by our senses. How much we need this grace! We ought all to think about it sometimes, because it is not at the moment we are to die, when perhaps our minds will be confused and stupefied, that we should begin to prepare for so great a favor. We ought to try to understand it while we can understand it, and then, when the awful moment comes, we shall know what the priest is doing, and by God's grace be able to receive this Sacrament in better dispositions.

We may then also receive the holy Viaticum; the word means something to go with us on a journey. It is the most holy Sacrament; it is Jesus HIMSELF who comes so mercifully and lovingly to go with us on our last journey—that terrible journey which we must all make some day or other.

And this is the only time which we can receive the holy Communion without fasting from midnight. See how good God is! He knows that when we are dying we may not be able to do without food or medicine, perhaps even for an hour, and so He allows us to receive the body and Blood of Jesus at any moment, that we may not go into His presence unprepared.

But it is probable that we may be with many persons who are to receive the last Sacraments before the awful moment when we shall receive them ourselves, and so I will say a few words about how we should help and prepare others.

When you are with any one who is very ill, you should beg of the doctor to tell you at once when there is the least danger. You should not wait until the person is actually dying, to send for the priest; but you must send at once when there is danger of death.

There are people who are so foolish, I had almost said "so wicked," that they will try to deceive themselves about their friends, and they will not listen or believe when the doctor tells them that there is danger. No one will die sooner for being prepared for death, and what will you say at the day of Judgment if through your fault your father, or mother, or brother, or sister, or child, or husband, has not been carefully prepared to meet God?

Again, people are afraid to tell their friends when they are dying. Now this is very, very wrong; if you are afraid to tell them yourself, get some one else to do it, but for the love of God, lose no time.

The room where a person is dying should be kept very quiet, and no gossiping should be allowed there; it is bad for any one who is very ill, and above all, it is bad for those whose minds should be free as far as possible from every distraction, and yet there are persons who, though they will not let the priest near their friends until the last moment, will let in every one else to keep up a noise and bustle, and crying, and clapping hands, which must do harm both to body and soul.

And at last, when the poor soul is just going to God to be judged, all should be perfectly quiet except one persen, and that one person should say some prayers, above all the Act of Contrition, and the Hail Mary, and if possible, the Recommendation for a Departing Soul, in a low, but clear tone of voice. You should not weary a sick or dying person with long prayers, for you might only confuse her mind; but you should say short prayers, and say them from time to time, just as you see the person can bear it; above all, you should say prayers after the poor soul has gone to the presence of God.

We should give our relations a quiet, respectable funeral, suitable to their station in life ; but never, never be so foolish as to spend money on a funeral, that would be better spent in getting Masses for the dead.

The grandest funeral in the world will not do the poor soul one bit of good, and may be the means of your committing sin of pride yourself. The Masses will benefit both yourself and the departed, because you will have a reward for your charity in getting them said.

You may perhaps think that the Sacrament of Holy Orders does not concern you in any way, and may consider that I should say nothing about it. But my children, what should we all do without priests? What would become of us if there were only two or three hundred priests in the world. instead of many thousands?

Do we ever think of the great debt of gratitude we owe to these good and holy men, who give up their lives to God's service? Can we ever do enough to repay them? And yet all they ask is that we should be good Christians ; that we should try to love and serve the good God, for whose love they have given up the pleasures of life; for whose love they go through so much weary toil and labor.

We ought to pray very often for those students who are preparing for the service of God in the different colleges throughout the world. My children, it is a grand thing to be a priest, but do not suppose it is an easy thing. See what these good young men give up for the love of God! Certainly He will give them a great and a most magnificent reward. Oh, my children, if we could only see the place that the good priests will get in Heaven, how we would honor them; but we do not see it, and they have to live by faith, like other Christians, and they have cares, and troubles, and trials, like every one else, and besides that, see what a hard life they live.

And yet it is when they are quite young that they choose this hard life. How God must love them, how the Angels must love them, and how we should reverence and respect them! It is indeed dreadful to hear people speaking lightly or disrespectfully of a priest.

My children, let no one ever tempt you to commit such a sin; even if a priest should happen to do wrong, it is not your place to judge him; he is God's anointed, and unless a priest should commit some dreadful sin, or leave the church, you should never speak of him with disrespect; and even then you should remember what he is, and pray for him.

You should listen to the advice of a priest with the greatest reverence. He knows what is right better than you do, and you may be sure you will never be sorry for doing what he tells you. It is only silly people who think they know more than any one else—who think themselves wiser than their superiors.

And now I have to say a few words about a very important Sacrament—the Sacrament of Matrimony. I suppose most girls wish to get married, and unless a girl has parents to support, for whose sake she remains single, or unless she has a hope that she may be a nun, there is no reason why she should not wish to be settled in life.

But this is a very serious matter, though, unfortunately, people are too fond of making a joke of it, and forgetting how much depends on making a good choice. People talk about getting married as if it were going out for a pleasure party; no wonder we hear of so many unhappy marriages, and so many very miserable homes!

My children, I beg of you to consider this subject well. It is certainly very foolish for a girl to be constantly thinking about getting married; but you must think of it sometimes, or, at all events, I am quite sure you will do so; therefore I am anxious to do what I can to help you to think the right way.

In the first place, when there is some talk about a girl getting married, or when you are asked to marry, you ought to pray to God to direct you. The peace and happiness of your whole future life may depend, and probably will depend, on the choice you make.

The first question you should ask is, if the man is a good, practical Catholic; a man who is not faithful to his God will not be faithful to his wife. A man who is not a good Christian will not be a good husband. Don't think so much about money, or settling yourself well in the world, but think a great deal about your soul, and about what will be good for you in the world to come.

Mind, I say, that any girl who marries a man given to drink, deserves the life of misery which is certain to be hers afterwards. If you walked of your own free inclination into a fire, no one would pity you if you were burned. You might say, "Oh, I will chance it; perhaps it won't burn me." And this is just the way some girls talk. They think because a young man is good-natured or good-looking, and above all, if he has a store and a few dollars, that it will be all right. They are sure they won't suffer, whoever else may.

Sometimes their friends warn them, and they won't listen. How often, unhappily, their friends urge them on, because it is a good match. Now it is you who will have to live all your life with this man, and not your friends. He may seem very fond of you now, and very goodnatured, but, my dear child, when had a drunkard a happy home? Never—never!

But you say you will reform him. A foolish, foolish idea; it is more likely he will pervert you. But you will say he only takes a little in drinking; a little is the sure and certain road to drinking to excess. If you are so anxious to marry this man, let him take the pledge, and if he keeps it for a year then you might venture; but if he does not, and if you are persuaded to marry him, you will repent it for the rest of your life.

No girl should ever meet young men at drinking-saloons, or go to such places. If you don't respect yourself, no one else will respect you. Take care of this. No good young man will care to marry a girl whom he sees going to such places.

Remember, also, that when you are married you must bear and forbear with each other. No one in this world is perfect; you are not perfect yourself, and you should not expect your husband to be perfect. If he should take to drink after you marry, it will be generally your own fault. If you make his home comfortable, he will stay there; if you don't, he will go elsewhere for the comfort and attention that you ought to give him.

Have his meals always ready for him, and always regular. Attend to any little thing that you know he wishes. Let him feel and see that you love him, and care for him more than for any one else in the whole world; and that you would be willing to sacrifice anything, or to do anything, for him. There are few married men who take to drink if they have really good wives. Pray for him and for yourself, every day, that you may have grace to fulfill all the duties of your state of life perfectly, and God's Holy Grace will be with you and with yours.

CHAPTER X.

ADVICE ABOUT GIVING GOOD EXAMPLE.

You will say, perhaps, "I am only a poor girl; how can I give good example?" But it is the duty of every one to give good example, and I wish to show you how you can do it, and to show you, also, that you may do a great deal more—both good and harm—than you think.

Example is like preaching a sermon without saying a word—a queer sermon, you will say; but listen, my children, I will tell you about a Saint who preached a sermon without saying a word. It was

St. Francis of Assisi, the Saint whose name I have the great happiness to bear, and to whose holy Order I have the great honor to belong.

He was born at a place near Rome, called Assisi; and as there are so many Saints of the name of Francis, he is known as St. Francis of Assisi. He was very wealthy, but he gave away all his money to the poor, and went about with an old habit on, and without shoes or stockings; in fact, looking just like a poor beggar. One day he said to some of his disciples: "Come, and let us preach a sermon;" and away they went. But he only walked about through the streets of the city, and came home, and never said a word.

"Father," said one of the monks, "you did not preach the sermon!"

"We did preach," said St. Francis, "for

we showed the people an example of poverty and humility."

Now this is the way we should all preach. Yes indeed, even people in the world can preach this way better than monks and nuns.

People expect nuns to wear a poor dress, and to be humble in their words and manner, and so they do not take so much notice of them in this way; but if they see a servant girl very modest in her manner, and dressed quietly, and regular at her religious duties, oh then they have something to say, and the good girl has preached a sermon, though she has never said a word.

Oh, how much good servants, and girls in an humble station of life may do if they would only try. Indeed, my children, you need not go into a convent to be saints or to do good; you can even be very good in the world, and you can do great, great things for God's glory and the good of souls.

Oh, think for one little moment how happy you will be at the day of Judgment, when some person says to you: "I thank you for the good example you gave me while we were on earth; it helped to make me good myself!" Or perhaps some one may even thank you for being the very means of her eternal salvation.

Masters and mistresses naturally watch their servants. They cannot help doing so, for so much depends on what they do, and say, and how they act. They will soon see if a servant does her duty honestly, and they will make their own remarks, though perhaps the girl may never hear them.

Those who are not Catholics will notice a Catholic servant or tradesman very much. They will say, "She believes her religion to be a better one than ours; now we shall see if she is any better than others!" Our Lord tells us Himself, that a tree must be judged by its fruit, and people do judge each other by what they do, not by what they say.

Now we know that the Catholic Church is Holy; we say every day in the Creed, "I believe in the Holy Catholic Church," but we know very well that it is the Church as a body which is Holy, and that there may be some very bad people in it. But Protestants do not think of this, and it is very hard to make them understand it. They say, "You talk about the Holy Catholic Church, but I had a Catholic servant once, and I assure you she was the laziest servant girl I ever knew, and I don't think she cared much for her religion either."

This may be quite true, and a very sad account this girl would have to give at the Day of Judgment for giving such bad example and bringing disgrace on her religion, but this does not make the Church one bit less Holy. There always was, and please God there always will be thousands and thousands of holy Catholics to atone for the sins of the careless and the wicked, and besides this the Church is Holy in her teaching, because she is taught by God, and Holy in her Sacraments because they are ordained by God.

But consider now what a good Catholic girl can do. Her mistress, if she is in service, or those who employ her, or her neighbors, would see that she was faithful to her religious duties, and to the duties of her state of life. The Catholic servant should be the best servant in the house. If she is not, the blame will too often be put on her religion by ignorant people, and what a dreadful thing this will be for her.

Again there are some Catholic servants who will make a great work about going to Mass and going to Confession, and talk a great deal about their religion, and yet they will give very bad example, for they will not do their duty well. What can people think? They will say, "That girl makes a great fuss about her religion, but I do not see that she is any better than other people." This is very bad.

Try, then, my children, to give good example for years; and years after, your conduct and your good example will be remembered and talked about. Perhaps some little child will have grown up to be a woman, and will be thinking about the true Faith, and will be inclined to become a Catholic. If you gave good example she will say, "I remember we had a Catholic servant; she was such a good girl, always regular at her business, and I know she thought a great deal of her religion, though she never said much about it, for she used to get up so early and get all her work well done when she wanted to go Mass or to Confession. How happy it will be for you if you have left this good impression of your religion, and remember that even very young children will notice things though you may not suspect it, and though they may not say a word at the time, they will think of it years and years after.

You should also avoid controversy. There are some Protestants who are never happy unless they are arguing about religion, and there are so many different opinions that they are always ready to change about from one to another, so that it is a sort of amusement to them to dispute

Of course all those different opinions cannot be right, and as they have no way of deciding which is right and which is wrong, all they they can do is to argue with each other. But it is very different with Catholics. We have a Religion and a Faith which was never altered, so we have only to believe what God teaches us by the Church.

Every Catholic ought to take great pains to know the doctrines of her religion well. At the present day, when people read so much and talk so much, a person may be asked questions. It is not difficult to see the difference. If you find that a person wants only to argue with you, that she may disturb your mind or insult your religion, you had better keep out of her way or be silent. You can say respectfully but firmly, that you do not wish to argue, for your mind is quite made up ; but if you find that a quiet word of explanation of any Catholic doctrine is wanted or asked for, then you should speak, and take care you know what you say.

This is very important, and Catholics so often take service with Protestant families, or live near neighbors to them, and are on friendly terms, that I shall add some remarks which may be useful in such cases, in the next chapter.

I have heard of several families who have been converted to the Catholic faith by the good example of their servants, and the good explanation which they gave of their religion.

Certainly, my children, we may not all be able to speak well or explain our Holy Faith well, but we can all give good example, and that is the best sermon we can preach.

We should also remember that we ought to be very patient and gentle when we hear others ridicule our religion. I am sorry to say there are some Protestants who do this, some Protestants who will torment their fellow servants with being "Papists" and "Irish." Now we need not to be ashamed either of our religion or our country, and if people revile us for either, that is no reason why we are to commit sin.

I am afraid there are some Catholics who defend their religion in a way that only does harm; who get angry when they are blamed about it, and sometimes give rude answers.

But this is not the way good Catholics should act. It is certainly right that we should be very earnest in the defence of our holy religion; that we should be ready to lay down our lives for it; that we should be ready to fight for it if it was necessary. But there are some persons who would sooner lay down their lives in the heat of battle, than lay down their tempers.

"What right has she to speak in that way of my religion?" This is what a girl will say sometimes, with a very cross face, and in a very angry tone of voice. No one has any right to speak against your religion and it is hard to listen to bitter and insulting words, and to accusations which you know are perfectly false. But this is no reason for you to lose your soul. However untrue the thing is that is said, the less reason why you should be angry; the more you should try to give good example, and to show that your religion teaches you to be very patient.

You may be quite sure that if you are quiet, and gentle, and patient, it won't go for nothing. In the first place, and this is of most consequence of all, it will please God. In the second place, there is nothing makes people so ashamed of being angry as giving them a gentle answer; and in the third place, though they may not say a word about it at the time, they will talk about it when their passion has cooled down, and they will say, "Well, there must be something in that girl's religion, for she never said an angry word, though I gave it to her well!"

My children, I am very anxious you should think about this. A good girl has a great deal of influence, and the more faithful, and humble, and holy she is, the more influence she will have. Now I hope every good girl will read this book, and there are two things I want you to do. First, I want you—each of you—to use all your influence to keep people from drink, and then I want you to use all your influence to keep them from quarrelling about religion.

You have brothers, and fathers, and friends who will be influenced by you, if you go about it the right way; not by talking a great deal, but by praying a great deal, and now and then you can put in a good word.

If you know any one who is tempted to drink, try and persuade him to go to a priest at once and take the pledge, even for a time. Men will often listen to a woman when they would not listen to any one else.

If you know people who are inclined to quarrel about religion, talk to them when you can get a quiet opportunity, and explain to them that this is not the best way to defend our holy faith.

I will tell you two stories, ones that I know to be true, and which happened in my own family.

Nearly all our servants were Catholics, and I must say, that they gave the very best example to my poor father and mother, who were Protestants; but we had a Protestant cook; she was a Welsh woman, and had a fearful temper. The coachman was a Catholic, and a really good servant, but he had a temper too, and now and then it got the better of him.

This woman used to take a wicked pleasure in teasing the man about his religion, and above all, when he would come in tired and hungry on a Friday, she would put a plate of the best meat she could get down before him, and then, when he would forget the day and eat it, she would laugh at him, and think she had done something very clever.

It was a cruel, wicked trick, but she was a bad, wicked woman, or else she was very bitter against Catholics, and this made her temper worse and worse, until she nearly got quite beyond control.

The poor fellow ate it readily several times, and always promised himself he would remember Friday, and that she should not trick him again; but she did trick him, for she laid herself out for it, and he got in a rage, and swore an awful oath if she ever did it again that he would take the knife she carved the meat with, and stick her through and through.

I need not tell you how very wrong he was. I tell you this story because, as I have said, I know it to be true, though it is many years ago since it happened. The man should have prayed for patience, and for a little memory, and if the woman had gone on trying him this way, he should have left his situation, no matter how well off he was.

No one should ever commit one sin to prevent another, and he should have remembered that he did not do wrong if he forgot that it was Friday.

But I am afraid he was as angry with the woman for teasing him, as he was for being made eat the meat; and I am afraid, also, that when people quarrel about religion, it is because they are angry at being taunted themselves, as much as for love of the faith.

Well, the next Friday the coachman came in again as usual, tired and hungry, and never thinking what day it was, the cook gave him meat. He remembered in a few minutes, and then he took up the knife to her, and I am afraid he might have killed her in his rage if she had not run upstairs into the drawing-room, where the guests were waiting for dinner to be announced.

He ran after her, and all the servants ran, and my father soon found out the cause; but though he was a Protestant, he would not allow injustice to be done to any servant in his house, and he told the cook if she ever dared to give the coachman meat again on a Friday, or anything that he should not eat, that he would turn her away from the house the next morning, so after that she was afraid.

Now if it had not been for God's mercy, a murder might have been committed, and think how dreadful it would have been if that man had killed a fellow creature in his rage. Alas! how many murders and how much "bad blood" is caused by disputing religion, the very last subject in the world about which people should quarrel.

You see, if the man had gone quietly to his master, it would all have been set right, and even if he had gone to him, and his master had taken the woman's part, he could have left his situation; better for him to have put himself out of the way of temptation, than to have run the risk of committing a dreadful sin.

To show what can be done by gentleness, I will tell you another story. We had another servant, a butler, some years after, who only staid with us a short time, and he went to be sacristan to a Catholic Church. This man happened to be with us during Lent, and on Good Friday he persuaded the whole family not to taste meat; he begged so hard, and spoke so beautifully about it, and asked how could any one refuse to fast on the day that Jesus died for us, that every one agreed except one lady. She had some meat cooked for herself, but she was taken ill suddenly, soon after dinner, and the very next day she had to get a doctor, and was nearly dying.

Thus you see what can be done by

gentleness and good example, and only at the last great Day, shall we know all that good Catholic servants have done, and how they have helped to convert sinners by their prayers and their good example.

CHAPTER XI.

ADVICE ABOUT SOME POINTS OF CONTROVERSY BETWEEN CATHOLICS AND PROTESTANTS.

When a girl can do so, she should always prefer service in a Catholic family. She may not get so good wages, or she may have harder work, but, as you will be well rewarded in Heaven for all you do on earth for the love of God, the loss of the wages will be made up to you there; and as you will be well rewarded for your work, the more you have to do the better, so as you do not injure your health.

But it will sometimes happen that a girl

must take service with Protestants, and then, indeed, she needs to give good example, and to be regular in her attendance at the Sacraments.

I would advise you, however, not to go into a Protestant family that you know to be very bitter against Catholics, for this reason: It is not right for any one to put herself in the way of temptations, and in such a family you would probably have great temptations.

There are some Protestants who will never let a Catholic girl alone, and this is no place for you. But again, there are Protestant families where you might be very comfortable, and not likely to injure your religion; and in such families you ought to do well.

One of the very first things that Protestants will attack a Catholic girl about is the Bible. Now this is really very amusing; for if it were not for Catholics, Protestants would have no Bible at all; yet they will say that Catholics do not care about the Bible.

I hope you will attend very carefully to the short explanations which I am going to give you, and that you will try to keep them in your mind. Only think, dear children, how happy it would be for you if you were the means of converting some Protestant to the one true Faith! Would it not be worth a little trouble? You cannot do much good unless you try to understand what you read, and then take some trouble. People will read a story very willingly, because it amuses them; but it is sometimes hard to get them to read a book which they may call "dry;" yet the story may do them very little good, and if it is bad may do them great harm, while the "dry" book may do them good; and thus they may do good to others, which may benefit them for all Eternity.

Now I will tell you how foolish this charge is against Catholics.

First: The Holy Apostles were Catholics, and our Lord told them to teach the Church, and they wrote in the Bible many of the instructions which our Lord gave to them—*but not all;* there were many things told to them which they were to teach others which are not in the Bible. But for all that, they loved and revered the Bible more than Protestants, for there are some parts of that part of the Bible called the Old Testament, which Protestants do not believe in, nor allow in their Bibles, and which are found in every

Catholic Bible; so, to begin with, Protestants have not the whole Bible.

In the next place, there are thousands of Protestants who do not believe in the Bible even as they have it. Luther, the founder of the Protestant religion, used to laugh at parts of the Protestant Bible.

Some Protestants talk a great deal about Luther having discovered the Bible, and that it never would have been known to people, only for Protestants. Now this is a falsehood. If Catholics had not kept the whole Bible carefully from the time of the Apostles to the present day, it would have been lost. It was monks and nuns who kept the Bible and made copies of it, before printing was found out, and this is a fact no one can deny.

Then, Protestants say that the priests will not allow Catholics to read the Bible.

This is not true. But the priests, or rather the Church to which the priests belong, will not allow us to read Protestant Bibles, because they are not the true Bibles, and not always correct translations, and do not contain the whole Bible.

Besides this, we are told in the Bible itself, that "*The unlearned and untaught wrest the Scriptures to their own destruction.*"—(2d Epistle of St. Peter, iii., 16.) "*And that no prophecy of Scripture is made by private interpretations.*"—(2d St. Peter, i., 20.) Now this is in the Protestant Bible as well as the Catholic, so even the Protestant Bible shows that the Church is right in not allowing people to interpret the Bible for themselves, but that they must take the interpretations of the Church, *because* the Church is appointed by God Himself, to teach us; and our

Lord Jesus Christ said Himself, "*He that heareth you, heareth me.*"—(St. Peter, v., 16.) And, "*If he will not hear the Church, let him be to thee as the heathen and the publican.*"—(St. Matt., xviii., 17).

It is quite certain that we cannot interpret a Bible for ourselves, for God has told us that we cannot; and it is also certain that Protestants who do try to interpret it never agree, and they cannot all be right. They are like the people in the Tower of Babel, who all spake different tongues. There are not two sects of Protestants who agree as to what they should believe, and when they do agree, it would be time enough for them to ask us to change.

Again Protestants constantly taunt Catholics with submitting to their priests and being led by them, and yet Catholics are only doing the very thing that the Bible tells them to do. Our Lord Himself says if we will not hear the Church, we are like the heathens and the publicans, and He left us in no doubt how to find out the Church, for He said to St. Peter:

"*Thou art Peter, and upon this rock I will build my Church, and the gates of Hell shall not prevail against it, and I will give to thee the Keys of the Kingdom of Heaven, and whosoever thou shalt bind upon earth it shall be bound also in Heaven, and whosoever thou shalt loose on earth it shall be loosed in Heaven.*"—(St. Matthew, xvi., 18–19.)

My children, how happy we are to belong to the Holy Catholic Church, which never has changed, and never can change, and believes not a part of the Bible, but the whole Bible; and above all, which has the power from God to release us from our sins.

Then Protestants will say "But how can a man forgive you your sins." Why this is the very thing the unworthy Jews said to our Lord Jesus Christ Himself. My children, a man cannot forgive us our sins of himself, by his own power or authority; but when God gives him power to do so, then he can forgive them, not in his own power, but by the power of God.

A King can forgive a murderer, but he does not do so himself; he sends the message through some one else. What a fool the man would be who would say, "I will not take this pardon unless the King gives it to me himself."

Again, Protestants say, "Oh, but you believe in good works, and you pray to saints and angels, and no one can save you but the Lord Jesus Christ." Poor Protestants! what a pity they will talk about what they do not understaud. A Protestant might be the most learned man in the world, and the cleverest man in the world, and yet a poor little beggar Catholic child might know, and perhaps would know, a great deal more.

All the learning in the world won't take people to Heaven, and the only true learning is what God teaches us ; for God alone knows everything, and what other people know is only guessing at the truth. But in religion there is no guessing. We Catholics are sure, for we are all taught by the Church, and we know that our Lord Jesus Christ left the authority to the Church to teach us, and this is told us in the Bible of which Protestants profess to be so fond, and yet they will not believe it.

The truth is that Protestants deceive themselves, and fancy they believe in the

Bible, whereas they only believe in what they fancy out of it—a bit here, and a bit there; but we Catholics believe it all, and love the whole Bible.

They accuse us of believing in good works, as if it was wrong to do so; and yet their own Bible would tell them that we must not only believe in good works, but *do them*.

The Apostle, St. James, says: "*What shall it profit, my brethren, if a man says he hath faith, but hath not works? shall faith save him?*"—(St. James ii., 14.) And again: "*So faith, also, if it have not works, is dead in itself.*"—(St. James ii., 17.)

And then this holy Apostle explains to us that the devils have faith, because they believe in God and tremble; yet what good does it do them? So that we cannot be saved without good works, as well as faith.

And, my children, I shall say a word of meaning to you here. There are, unhappily, some Catholics who say, "Oh, I shall be all right; at least I belong to the true Church; I shall certainly be saved;" and they live very bad and even wicked lives. My children, this kind of faith will not save them. You might believe all the doctrines of the holy Church, and go to Hell. You must do good works—not because good works of themselves will save you, but because the tree is known by its fruit. You do not love God unless you do what He commands you, and you cannot go to Heaven unless you love God.

Luther, the real founder of the Protestant religion, was a bad, wicked man, and so, of course, he wrote and spoke against good works; and, unhappily, many Protestants, who are not wicked as he was, followed his bad teaching, instead of the teaching of the Bible.

Protestants say, "Oh, I believe in the Lord Jesus Christ, and He will save me!" It is very hard to know what Protestants mean by saying they believe in the Lord Jesus Christ. The devils believe in Him also, but that does not save them; but if they truly believed in our Lord they would believe all He taught. And it was He Himself who told us that we were to hear the Church, and that we were to get pardon of our sins by absolution from the priest. Now, if people do not believe this, they do not really believe in the Lord Jesus Christ, whatever they may say; it is not saying we believe, but doing what we are told, that will ensure our Eternal Salvation.

Again, Protestants say that we pray to the Saints and Angels. Well, so we do; but Protestants think that we worship them as we worship God, which we do not do. Now Protestants are very unjust and unfair to Catholics; it is their own loss, and we ought to be very sorry for them, but *never angry*.

I know it is very bad to have Protestants bring the same charge against us again and again, and saying we worship the Saints, and pray to them in place of God, when we have told them again and again that we do *not*. If any one should taunt you thus, the best plan is to be silent. When you have quietly explained what you do, and what you do not do, if they will not believe you it will be because they do not choose to believe you, so just let them alone. The loss is their own; you have done your duty, and if you get angry you only commit a sin, and this is all that the devil wants.

Just say, quietly, "Well, if you do not believe my word, there is no use in saying any more;" and you may be sure that this quiet answer and your own silence will do far more good than all the arguments you could use.

You know very well that you only ask the prayers of the Saints and Angels, just as you would ask the prayers of any good person in this world. Every time a priest says Mass he asks the people to pray for him; and if we ask our sinful fellow-creatures, who are in this world, to pray for us, how much more should we not ask those who are with God in Heaven, and who must be able to pray so much better for us than when they were on earth?

We are told in the Bible by our Lord Himself, that the devil knows all that is going on in this world, and so do the holy Angels. In the parable of the rich man and Lazarus we find this, and we find that the holy Angels know what we say and do.

And then as to holy relics. Relics are constantly mentioned in the Bible as the means employed to work miracles. We are told in the Acts of the Apostles:

"*That God wrought by the hand of Paul more than common miracles, so that even there were brought from his body to the sick, handkerchiefs and aprons, and the diseases departed from them, and the wicked spirit went out of them.*"

We should remember the words, "*God*

wrought;" it was God Himself who gave the relics their virtue, as it is only God who can give virtue to the relics of the saints.

It is therefore silly and unmeaning for Protestants to talk as if we worshipped saints as the heathen worship false gods, or as if we put the saints in the place of God. It is God Himself who has given the saints power to work miracles; it is He Himself who has told us, even in the Bible, that He has given this power to His saints.

When our Lord Jesus Christ was making His last solemn discourse to His chosen Disciples, on the very night before He was crucified, He told them this. In the Gospel of St. Mark, we read that our Lord appeared to His disciples after He had risen from the dead, and said to them: "And these signs shall follow them that believe: They shall cast out devils, they shall speak with new tongues,

"They shall take up serpents, and if they shall drink any deadly thing, it shall not hurt them; they shall lay their hands upon the sick, and they shall recover."—(St. Mark xvi., 17–18.)

You see by this that we are to expect miracles, and you know that it is only in the holy Catholic Church that miracles occur; so it is no wonder that Protestants say they do not believe in them, for there are none in their own church; it is only to God's church that the power of working miracles is given.

We also read in the Acts of the Apostles, of all the miracles worked by the saints of those days, and how even the very shadow of St. Peter worked miracles, so that sick people were laid in the street, that his shadow might fall upon them as he passed along, and cure them.

And my children, miracles are still taking place every day in the church of God.

I hope to write another book for you, with some account of the wonderful lives, and the great miracles which have been performed in our times.

It is true that Protestants will not believe these miracles; but my children, this does not make them less true. We read in the Holy Gospels that the unbelieving Jews though they saw our Lord's miracles with their own eyes; they even tried to kill Him, because He worked such great miracles, and St. John, the beloved disciple of Jesus, says:

"*And whereas he had done so many*

miracles before them, they believed not in him."—(St. John xii., 37.)

So we need not wonder if people now will not believe the miracles done by God's saints. But though people will not believe these things, they will believe lies and superstitions; yet it is a fact that while Protestants are undoubtedly taunting Catholics with being superstitious, and believing what is not true, they are themselves the real superstitious people, for they believe in table-turning and spirit-wrapping, and all these things, which can only be done by the power of the devil, and with which no Catholic should have anything to do.

We know that God allows the devil to have a great deal of power, and that he can do anything to deceive people and lead them away from the truth, and this is one of the very things which he tries to deceive people by now. Those who will not beleive in God's saints, and the miracles worked by them, are allowed, with great justice, to believe in the devil and the wonders that he can do.

CHAPTER XII.

ADVICE ABOUT DEVOTIONS TO OUR BLESSED LADY.

One thing I am sorry to say that some Protestants seem to like much, is to argue about the devotions which Catholics offer to the Mother of God, and sometimes they say such things that it is hard indeed to keep from being very angry. But, my children, the humble and gentle Mother of Jesus was never angry—never, even in her whole blessed life ; and when we know how the Son of God, her only child Jesus, was scourged and persecuted by wicked men; and when we think of what she felt and suffered about this, we see what a great example she has given us, and how earnestly we should try to follow it.

We can never be provoked as she was. Besides, as I said before, we ought to be sorry for those unhappy people, instead of being angry with them; and when people go about giving lectures against the Catholic religion, we should keep away from such places, and take no notice of the people who do it, for they are only encouraged to go on when they find that Catholics will go to such places, even to oppose them.

Leave them to God. He will judge them; we can only pray for them, and try to atone to God for their sins. It may please us for the time to go to such places even, to hear those who speak in them, but it will not please God, and the more God is displeased by such wicked people, the more we should do to please Him and console Him for their sins. This is what is called making compensation.

It is just as if we had a friend who had suffered a great deal of wrong from a bad, ungrateful son or daughter, and we loved this friend so much, that the more she suffered the more we tried to repair, or make up to her for the wrong that had been done her.

We cannot have too much love and devotion to the Mother of Jesus. The very fact that she is His Mother should be enough of itself to make us love her. And if the Saints can do so much for us— can help us so much by their prayers, and even work miracles for us by their relics, how much more can the Mother of God do, who was the only sinless woman! She works miracles of grace every day for us poor sinners; she prays for the wicked and the miserable, and she never fails any one who trusts her, however humble, however poor. We have only to ask her, and she hears us at once, and prays for us to her Divine Son, and we know He cannot refuse her anything she desires.

Let us then have great confidence in our Blessed Lady, and let us show her the best kind of devotion—that of imitating her holy example. Let us try to be like her. She was poor, but she was content with her poverty. She suffered a great deal—far more than any one of us can ever suffer, but she never complained. Her whole life was devoted to the service of God, and she neither cared for, nor thought about, this poor world, except so far as she could help sinners to get to that better world which shall be Eternal.

Pray to her often, my children; ask her to be your mother; you will never regret the confidence you place in her.

And I would especially recommend you to wear the Scapular, and to be enrolled in the Confraternity of the Scapular; by doing this you place yourself in a special manner under the protection of our Blessed Mother Mary, and you obtain her special help at the hour of death, when you will need it most.

My children, I must now bid you goodbye for the present. I hope, if God spares my life, to write another book for you soon.

Pray for me, and I will promise to pray for you; indeed, I have already prayed often for every one who shall read this "Good Advice."

Sister Mary Frances Clare,
Convent of Poor Clares,
Kenmare, County Kerry,
Ireland.

Feast of the Immaculate Conception, 1871.

COPY OF A LETTER

Sent by our Illustrious Pontiff, Pius IX, to Sister Mary Francis, the writer of this good little book.

[Translation.]

To our Beloved Daughter in Christ, Mary Francis Clare, of the Sisters of Saint Clare, Kenmare.

PIUS P.P. IX.

BELOVED DAUGHTER in Christ, Health and Apostolic Benediction. We congratulate you, Beloved Daughter in Christ, on having completed a long and difficult work which seemed to be above woman's strength, with a success that has justly earned the applause of the pious and the learned. We rejoice, not only because you have promoted by this learned and eloquent volume the glory of the illustrious Apostle of Ireland, St. Patrick, but also because you have deserved well of the whole Church; for in recording the actions of so great a man you have placed before the eyes of the world the benefits received through the

Catholic religion so clearly that they can no longer be questioned. For not only did he bring the light of faith to a people that sat in darkness and the shadow of death, but he reclaimed and civilized their wild and barbarous customs, so that the island became entirely changed, and was justly styled the Island of Saints. The clergy appointed by him throughout the land, together with being remarkable for faith and piety, devoted themselves also to the study and advancement of science. And when the rest of Europe was wasted by barbarous hordes, and overpowered with ignorance and darkness, your country was the sure refuge of literature and scholarship, and received with welcome the youth that crowded to her shores, and sent out very many men, most distinguished for learning and piety, to be the apostles of various nations. Now, for so great a gift, Ireland was indebted to this Apostolic See, because St. Patrick taught no other faith except that which was handed down here; and which, from the very beginning of Christianity, having raised up the nations that were enslaved by superstitions and error, and sunk down in the foul mire of sensual indulgence, bound them together in love, and reduced them to those habits of life which are worthy of man's dignity. While these facts refute most clearly the false charges of ignorance, darkness, and opposition to progress which are not unfrequently brought against the Church and this Holy See, the Life of St. Patrick, as written so carefully by you, has the further merit of pointing out this benefit to every one, and the more forcibly and effectively because this result flows naturally from the narrative. But as we look with wonder at the abiding fruits of this most holy prelate's mission, evidenced by the constancy of your nation in the faith, never shaken by persecution, violence, fraud, or affliction, for so many ages, we have every ground to trust that this most pious people will be still more encouraged to tread in the footsteps of their ancestors, by having placed before them anew the memory of former glorious deeds. We certainly augur this successful issue from your labor; and at the same time we impart to you and to your sisters, most lovingly, the Apostolic Benediction, as an earnest of God's favor and a pledge of Our goodwill.

Given at Rome, at St. Peter's, the 6th October, 1870, the Twenty-fifth year of Our Pontificate.

PIUS P.P. IX.

www.ingramcontent.com/pod-product-compliance
Lightning Source LLC
Chambersburg PA
CBHW032226230426
43666CB00033B/1608